THE
KNITTING
POCKET BIBLE

THE
POCKET BIBLE
SERIES

The Allotment Pocket Bible

The Baking Pocket Bible

The Camping Pocket Bible

The Cat Lover's Pocket Bible

The Christmas Pocket Bible

The Cook's Pocket Bible

The Cricket Pocket Bible

The Dad's Pocket Bible

The DIY Pocket Bible

The Dog Lover's Pocket Bible

The Football Pocket Bible

The Gardener's Pocket Bible

The Golf Pocket Bible

The Jane Austen Pocket Bible

The Knitting Pocket Bible

The London Pocket Bible

The Mum's Pocket Bible

The Outdoor Pocket Bible

The Pregnancy Pocket Bible

The Railway Pocket Bible

The Traveller's Pocket Bible

The Wedding Pocket Bible

The Wine Pocket Bible

THE
KNITTING
POCKET BIBLE

MIMI HILL

This edition first published in Great Britain 2011 by
Crimson Publishing, a division of Crimson Business Ltd
Westminster House
Kew Road
Richmond
Surrey
TW9 2ND

A catalogue record for this book is available from the British Library.

ISBN 978 1 907087 226

Typeset by IDSUK (DataConnection) Ltd
Printed and bound by L.E.G.O. SpA, Trento

ACKNOWLEDGEMENTS

To the most Smashing Puffin.

This book wouldn't have been made possible without the help and support of the wonderful knitting community and readers of my blog. Many thanks to Saffron, who warmed my hands whilst I typed; to Vivianne for the constant support, the yarn and the chocolate; to Vera, for the amazing diversions; and to Lisa and Steph, for their friendship and love. Many thanks to the wonderful Skein Queen for entrusting me with yarn for the scarf in this book.

Thank you to Craig, for the support.

CONTENTS

INTRODUCTION

Knitting is an old skill that has found a new following. Where once people would have knitted out of the necessity to clothe their families, a new generation of knitters have now picked up their needles to knit for pleasure and for the joy of creating something personal and handmade.

No longer created mainly for function, many modern knits have a new excitement, almost a frivolity, with fresh shapes and innovative materials making the act of knitting a pleasurable past time as well as a link back to a past heritage where such skills were an essential part of life.

From chunky, sculptural knitwear to the cobweb-weight lace knit in the most delicate and intricate patterns and yarn, there has never been so much variety in knitting as there is today. The range of innovative yarns now on the market can transform even the simplest garter stitch scarf into a work of art.

Knitters have thrown out the image of knitting as being the preserve of little, grey-haired old ladies, slowly churning out a production line of baby bootees for their brood of grandchildren. Nowadays you may find teenage granddaughters knitting alongside their grandmothers, and proud fathers knitting for their families.

The Knitting Pocket Bible is intended as a trusty companion for knitters of all generations. As well as a handy knitting guide it is packed full of fun facts and trivia, advice and ideas. We've even included some knitting patterns to keep your needles entertained.

ESSENTIAL EQUIPMENT

As with most hobbies, the further enthralled an enthusiast becomes with their topic, the more equipment and gadgetry they seem to acquire. Knitting is not particularly different in this regard, but it requires little equipment – just some yarn and needles – to begin with. Having said that, the acquisition of new tools and gadgets to make knitting easier and more pleasurable is part and parcel of the transition from 'someone who can knit' into 'a knitter'. This chapter will guide you through all of the essential equipment you need to get started, as well as describing a few of the more exotic pieces of kit.

KNITTING NEEDLES

Knitting needles come in a great variety of forms and materials – the traditional long, pointy stick with a bead-like finial on the end being the most instantly recognisable type. Other types of knitting needles include:

- **Circular needles**. These are two short needle points connected by a flexible cable, and are used for knitting 'in the round': a technique which allows the knitter to create seamless cylindrical tubes of knitted fabric for items such as hats or sleeves.

- **Double pointed needles**. Also called 'DPNs', these are short needles with a point on each end, sold in sets of four or five. They are used for knitting small-diameter objects in the round, and are particularly useful for socks and small soft toys.

KNITTING NEEDLE MATERIALS

There is even greater variety in the materials that knitting needles might be manufactured from. Many knitting needles manufactured in the 1970s and 1980s were of two types – grey powdered-steel needles, and needles made from brightly coloured plastic. Both of these types are still manufactured and available to buy, but have fallen from popularity with the recent resurgence of knitting as a hobby, as a new generation of knitters seek to improve both the comfort and functionality of the tools they choose.

Materials used for modern knitting needles include the following:

Powder-coated steel

Inexpensive, relatively heavy needles with a high amount of 'grip'. Some knitters find that the amount of drag caused by the needles slows down their knitting, as stitches waiting to be knitted do not work their way down the needle so readily. Conversely, some knitters may find this beneficial when working with very slippery fibres such as silk.

Nickel-plated

Smooth, shiny metal needles, which allow the stitches to glide over them for the ultimate experience in speed knitting. Some knitters find the 'slipperiness' of these needles to be too much, with stitches accidentally slipping off the needles when using yarns such as silk or bamboo.

Acrylic

Smooth, slightly flexible needles with a medium amount of grip. Acrylic needles are often very light in comparison to metal needles, making them easy to take on the move.

Bamboo

Lightweight and slightly flexible, with a relatively high amount of grip. The bamboo absorbs oil from the knitter's hands over time and many people find that the needles 'improve' with continued use.

Pocket Tip
Some knitters with arthritic conditions report that the warmth of the bamboo makes knitting less painful, allowing them to knit for greater lengths of time.

Wood

Wooden needles are manufactured from many different varieties of wood and are often very beautiful. Most types of wooden needles have a medium amount of grip and similar warmth properties to bamboo needles, but with less flexibility.

Glass

The beauty of glass needles is under no debate, but the practicality of knitting with two glass sticks definitely is. Wonderful to look at as a display piece, glass needles are cold in the hands, heavy, inflexible, noisy, and often 'catch' as the two needles meet.

Casein

Made from milk protein, casein needles are smooth, flexible and will absorb warmth from the hands with use. As with bamboo needles, these properties may be beneficial to knitters with arthritic or rheumatic conditions.

NEEDLE SIZES

Knitting needles come in a wide variety of sizes, from the almost wire-thin to giant needles with the circumference of a broomstick. The size of the knitting needles used to create a piece of fabric is one of the most important determining factors in the nature and properties of the finished item. As a general rule, the thicker the yarn, the larger the needles, but designers will often go against this convention to lend new properties to their designs. Super-fine lace weight yarns knitted on large needles will create very airy fabric with a fantastic amount of drape. Bulky yarn knitted on small needles will, conversely, create a very dense, stiff fabric.

Pocket Fact ☺

In 2006, a knitter from Cornwall broke the world record for knitting with the world's largest needles, creating a 10-stitch-wide tension square using needles 6.5cm in diameter and 3.5m long.

FINDING THE RIGHT SIZE NEEDLES

Knitting patterns will almost always specify a needle size intended to work with the pattern, given in one of three formats:

- Metric measurements (given as the diameter of the needle in millimetres)
- US needle sizes
- UK needle sizes

Unfortunately, needle sizing varies greatly on either side of the Atlantic. The UK system uses higher numbers to denote finer needles, while the American knitting needle manufacturers use a system that assigns incrementally larger numbers to larger-sized needles, meaning UK knitters have ended up with a system that is almost the exact reverse of the American way of doing things.

Adding to this already confusing dual-system is a lack of distinct industry standardisation on what measurement a particular size needle should actually be. Some American needle manufacturers produce their size 2 needles at a measurement of 2.75mm, whereas others make them to measure 3mm.

Pocket Tip ✁

One way to avoid some of the transatlantic confusion over needle sizing is to use the metric system of measurements. Whereas manufacturers have some flexibility in what they class as a 'size 7', metric measurements are a scientifically defined standard and 5mm is and will always be the same measurement, no matter where you are in the world.

A useful tool to help ensure you select the right sized needle for your project, in cases where the numbering system on your knitting needles does not match that of the pattern you are referring to, is a needle gauge (see page 25), along with a handy needle size conversation chart.

NEEDLE SIZE CONVERSION CHART

Metric (mm)	US needle size	UK needle size
1.75	00	15
2	0	14
2.25	1	13
2.5	1½	—
2.75	2	12
3	2½	11
3.25	3	10
3.5	4	—
3.75	5	9
4	6	8
4.25	6	—
4.5	7	7
5	8	6
5.5	9	5
6	10	4
6.5	10½	3
7	—	2
7.5	—	1
8	11	0
9	13	00
10	15	000

A good selection of needles

One of the questions most often posed by relatively new knitters is what size and type of needles to invest in. Many knitters start by learning to knit using traditional straight needles, as these are most familiar to them. The first pair of knitting needles should suit the weight of the yarn. The ball band will give a good indication of the needle size most often required to give a good smooth fabric which is neither too loose nor too dense (see page 19 for a sample ball band).

Beginners should start with a cheap and durable, fairly thin yarn such as DK weight acrylic or wool/acrylic blend, with 4mm or 5mm needles, so you can practise with something easy to unpick and re-knit while you're still learning, and not damage a more expensive yarn. By using mid-size needles you will also be able to see the stitches more easily as your knitting will be quite compact and neat.

After this, a compulsion to buy new needles for every project will start to make itself apparent. When you calculate how many different types of needles there are available (at least 21 sizes in each form of needle – straights, DPNs and then circulars, which come with a wide range of different cord lengths) the range of possible tools can seem expensive and daunting.

One relatively recent innovation in knitting-needle technology is the development of interchangeable circular needles. These needle sets are particularly handy as they comprise the most popular sizes of needle tips as well as flexible cables of various lengths, which either screw or clip on to the needle tips to give the knitter a wide range of circular needle sizes and lengths. Circular needles can also be used for 'flat' knitting (knitting back and forth in rows, rather than in the round), and a technique known as Magic Looping also allows circular needles to be used in lieu of DPNs for small-diameter knitting. Though an interchangeable needle set can sometimes seem like a large outlay to begin with, many knitters will never need to buy another knitting needle, so they often prove to be a great money-saver in the long run and are very easy to use.

 YARN

Yarn is the stuff that many knitters live for. Far from the tradi-tional view of yarn (often indiscriminately and incorrectly called 'wool'), yarn is now produced from materials as varied and diverse as seashells, milk protein and plastic bags. In fact, anything that can be manipulated into a long, thin, flexible strand can be knitted.

With such a vast choice of materials to knit with it can be daunt-ing trying to decide which yarn is suitable for which project. Many knitters enjoy experimenting with various yarns and small projects, where if the match is not particularly suitable neither yarn nor time is wasted in too great measure. However, each material has particular qualities that may make it particularly suitable for certain projects, and a terrible choice for others (though some recipients may cherish a pair of itchy Icelandic wool underpants).

TYPES OF YARN AND THEIR QUALITIES

Understanding the characteristics of different fibres can help the knitter make informed yarn choices and successfully match a yarn type to a project.

Wool

Probably the best-known knitting material, 'wool' can be obtained from a number of different animals, but in a knitting context it is a term most often used to refer specifically to the wool of a sheep.

Not all wool is equal. In fact, this is far from the case. Wool is graded according to its length, softness and sheen. The finest wool comes from the merino sheep (see page 9 for further infor-mation on this particular fibre), and can range from the almost buttery softness of this breed, to the coarse, almost 'crunchy' tex-tured wool of sheep with hardier coats – mostly used for mattress filling and carpeting.

Pocket Fact 😊

Many sheep bred for meat stock do not produce wool suitable for any form of textile use.

Wool is distinguishable from fur or hair as found on other mammals due to several characteristics of its construction. It is very elastic along the length of each strand and is 'crimped'. Wool's natural characteristics also allow for an almost magical transformation to take place when heat, water and agitation are applied to the knitted fabric. The strands of fibre contract and the microscopic scales along the shaft of each strand interlock and bond together, producing a wonderfully thick felt through the process of 'fulling' (a term specifically used for the act of felting pre-knitted fabrics). This property can be utilised to create some absolutely wonderful items, such as thick, hardwearing slippers. It can also prompt the onset of tears, heartache and a string of expletives if the process is inadvertently applied to a favourite pure wool jumper, accidentally caught up in a machine wash.

Wool in both its knitted and felted forms is a fabulous insulator, trapping warm air between the individual fibres and keeping the body's own generated heat close to the skin — making it the perfect material for winter-weather wear.

Wool allergies

Though wool has been used to clothe humans for many centuries, many people find they are allergic to wool. Some people have an allergy to lanolin— from the Latin lana *(wool), and* oleum *(oil) — a waxy substance secreted by the sebaceous glands of sheep. Many more people, though not actually allergic to either wool or lanolin, find that they are sensitive to wool — perhaps a hangover from itchy school jumpers and uncomfortable winter hats.*

When knitting for people with wool allergies or sensitivities it is advisable to enquire what fibres the intended recipient chooses when they shop for clothes and to look for projects suited to those fibres. Alpaca (see page 12) is a good alternative to wool for many people as it does not contain the lanolin which cause allergies in some wearers.

Superwash wool

Wool which has undergone the Superwash treatment is easier to care for than un-treated wool, as the microscopic outside scales of the fibres are removed in a chemical process, meaning that the fibres are smoother and so do not 'lock' together so readily. This means there is less likelihood of accidental felting during washing, or from agitation and wear. Superwash wool is a good choice for knitters who want an easy-care garment without resorting to man-made fibres.

Merino

Merino wool comes from a breed of sheep bred primarily for the fineness of its wool and the high value of its much sought-after fibre. Selective breeding of fine-coated sheep from foundation flocks bred in the 12th and 13th centuries has resulted in modern merino sheep being prized for their wonderful fleeces. Prior to the 18th century, merino wool was so highly valued in Spain that it was a crime punishable by death to be found exporting merino sheep to foreign lands. Today most merino wool originates from Australia and New Zealand (where sheep outnumber human inhabitants 12:1 – a knitter's paradise) but the production of merino wool is not without its opponents.

Mulesing

Mulesing is a controversial practice that helps to protect the merino sheep from parasitic flystrike, a painful condition in which the burrowing larvae of certain flies find a host in the skin and tissue of living sheep. Merino sheep are particularly susceptible due to folds of wool-laden skin, which have been developed through selective breeding to produce as high a yield per head of sheep as possible for the farmers. Mulesing is a preventative measure involving the removal of the folds of skin from around the breeches (the bottom) of the sheep. Though many sheep farmers deem this surgical procedure necessary to prevent a particularly nasty and painful condition, it is itself a very painful experience for the sheep, and as such has come under scrutiny from many animal welfare groups.

The properties of merino wool are mostly the same as those of wool, but with the added luxury of an extremely soft, non-itchy fibre which, though extremely warm, has an almost 'cool' feel against the skin due to the smoothness of its fine fibres.

Acrylic

One of a range of man-made fibres, acrylic is inexpensive, readily available and easy to care for. Invented by DuPont in 1941 and rising to prominence in the 1960s and 1970s, spun acrylic soon became known as a wonder fibre: easy to care for, hard-wearing and (unlike wool) suitable to be thrown in the washing machine. Acrylic does not shrink, can be tumble-dried and, as the colour is added to the polymer before it is turned into fibre (rather than being dyed afterwards), it does not run. Despite these qualities it is no longer a universally admired fibre however, and instead polarises opinion quite drastically.

Many people now see acrylic as a cheap, undesirable material. Complaints about the yarn actually 'squeaking' whilst being knitted are a common grievance, along with the complaint that once wet it refuses to be blocked (see pages 73–75) or otherwise manipulated into shape, and that heat does not escape from the knitted fabric at all, causing sweating and discomfort. Chief among its negative points, though, seems to be the simple fact that it is plastic. In an age where knitters practise their craft not because they have to knit to clothe their family, but for enjoyment and to look to the traditions of a natural and homemade way of life, there seems to be no room for this once 'wonder fibre' in many knitters' yarn stash.

Nylon

Another of DuPont's man-made fibre innovations, nylon is a silky, lustrous fibre, well known for its uses in the production of women's hosiery. There are only a few 100% nylon knitting yarns on the market, as nylon is mostly found blended with other fibres to give strength and longevity to natural yarns. It is most commonly found in sock yarns, where a small amount (20% or so) is added to provide strength and resistance to wear in areas such as sock heels and toes, which are often 'rubbed' due to the friction of walking in shoes.

Cotton

The fluffy fibres of the cotton plant have been harvested for centuries for use in textile manufacture. Cotton produces a cool, breathable fabric, perfect for summer use. Cotton has very little 'give' and as such may be unsuitable for items designed to hug the limbs, or stay up (such as socks) unless a proportion of elastane is added to the blend when spinning. It is this same lack of give that presents a challenge to some knitters, as the inelasticity of the yarn can make tight stitches difficult to knit.

Relatively easy to care for, cotton can be blocked into shape but tends to suffer from sagging after extended wear due to the weight and inelasticity of the fibres.

Pocket Fact ☺

During medieval times people were surprised to find that the cotton fibres that were being imported from Asia were plant-based. The fibres were so similar to the fluffy white fibre of sheep it was decided that the fibres must be sheared from plant-borne sheep. This belief is summed up by John Mandeville, writing in 1350: 'There grew in India a wonderful tree which bore tiny lambs on the ends of its branches. These branches were so pliable that they bent down to allow the lambs to feed when they are hungrie.'

Silk (mulberry or cultivated)

Obtained from the cocoons of the larvae of the mulberry silkworm *Bombyx mori*, silk is a protein fibre with a lustrous sheen and extremely high tensile strength. Its smooth but non-slippery surface gives a very lightweight drape to fabrics and has been highly prized as a fabric for many hundreds of years. Silk is a poor conductor of electricity and as such can be subject to electrostatic clinginess, though it is this same property that allows it to trap warm air in cool climates. Its absorbency also means that silk is a comfortable fabric to wear in warmer temperatures, so the old adage of silk keeping you cool in the summer and warm in the winter is partly true. Pure silk yarns can be relatively pricey, but affordable silk blend yarns allow for the luxury of a touch of silk without the added price tag. Animal lovers may want to consider 'wild silk' instead though, given the manufacturing process used to create cultivated silk (see below).

Silk (tussah or wild)

Tussah and other types of 'wild' silk are sometimes known as 'peace silk' due to their cruelty-free methods of production. Wild silk cocoons from caterpillars (other than the mulberry silk moths used in cultivated silk production) are gathered after the newly formed moths have hatched and left their silken temporary home. Unlike in cultivated silk manufacture, the process is organic and moths are not killed in the process. As the moth is allowed to hatch, the cocoon is broken and split open, breaking the silk filament into much shorter lengths than the 1,500m that can be obtained from an unbroken mulberry silk cocoon. Tussah silk is not believed to be as fine or luxurious as cultivated silk, but for some people the organic manufacturing process makes up for the tiny amount of lustre lost from the silk.

Alpaca

The long, lustrous fibres of the camelid alpaca are valued for their sheen, softness and warmth. Unlike sheep's wool, alpaca fibre contains no lanolin, making it hypoallergenic and a possible alternative fibre choice for those who find that they are sensitive to wool.

Cashmere

Fibre obtained from the cashmere goat is highly prized and can be rather expensive. Cashmere goats grow a coat that is 'double-haired', meaning that it has two layers of fibre: coarser guard hairs and the softer, luxurious fibres that are so coveted by knitters and clothing manufacturers.

Pocket Fact ☺

There are a number of stringent rules that cashmere producers must abide by to be able to call their fibre 'cashmere'. The fibre must be free from any guard hairs, which are not considered to be cashmere, even though they originate from the fleece of the cashmere goat. No more than 3% of the fibres may exceed 30 microns in diameter, and the whole sample must be 19 microns or less on average. These strict guidelines ensure that properly assessed cashmere is always a luxury purchase, and usually quite a pricey one.

Mohair

Fibre sourced from the Angora goat is known as mohair (confusingly, angora fibre comes from Angora rabbits). A luxury fibre, mohair is lustrous and has a good amount of sheen to it. Often found blended with other fibres to add luxury and a lofty halo to a yarn blend, mohair is warm and can be quite 'fuzzy' in appearance.

Angora

Angora yarn comes from the Angora rabbit, rather than the Angora goat (the hair from the goat is known as mohair, just to confuse knitters). Angora is an incredibly soft and fuzzy fibre and is also extremely warm and squishy.

Angelic yarn?

Angora yarn has a very noticeable 'halo' to it (fuzzy ends of individual fibres that lie at right angles to the main strand of yarn) which trap air, making it extremely warm. This halo also catches the light (hence the name) and produces a slight tickling sensation that some people love and which drives other people crazy. This same halo can sometimes obscure individual stitches, which means some knitters find angora difficult to work with.

Rayon (viscose, Modal, Tencel)

Neither a natural nor a fully synthetic fibre, rayon has been termed a semi-synthetic yarn as it uses naturally occurring polymers found in materials such as wood pulp to create an essentially man-made yarn through industrial processes. The finished yarn product is so far removed from its natural origins that it cannot be said to be 'natural' in the same way that wool or cotton are. Despite this, rayon does not feel at all plastic-like to the touch, blocks well, has a high level of sheen and drape and is extremely absorbent, wicking moisture away from the body and making it particularly suitable for summer-wear.

Bamboo

Items labelled 'bamboo' are usually bamboo-derived rayon (see rayon, page 14). Many yarn companies producing bamboo-based rayon praise the sustainability of the fast-growing, easily harvested bamboo plant, but some green campaigners have criticised the levels of harsh and potentially environmentally unfriendly chemicals used in the production of the fibre. Sharing many properties with other rayon yarns, bamboo-based rayon is extremely absorbent with a high level of drape when knitted.

Pocket Fact ☺

Some producers of bamboo yarn are also very keen to promote the claimed antibacterial properties of the yarn, sometimes touting them as combating sweat odour, but these claims are yet to be scientifically proven.

Linen

Fabrics and yarn produced from the fibres of the flax plant are known as 'linen'. Among the strongest of the plant fibres, linen is two to three times more robust than cotton. It is highly absorbent, and can absorb up to 20% of its own weight in water before it begins to feel damp. Linen dries very readily, and sweat is wicked away from the body – perfect for warm weather garments.

YARN CONSTRUCTION

Fibre content is not the only factor that goes towards giving a yarn its 'character'. How the yarn is spun and plied are also determining factors in the eventual look and behaviour of the yarn and fabric.

Single ply

A single ply or singles yarn is a solitary length of yarn that has been twisted into a strand and is available in many weights, from lace to bulky. Due to the single-ply construction of this yarn, it can be relatively weak and will 'pull apart' if knitted at too high a tension. Depending on the amount of twist added to the yarn and the stitch pattern used, singles yarns can sometimes bias, causing a piece of knitting to slant at a diagonal if it isn't blocked.

Plied yarns

The majority of yarn found for sale is plied in construction, meaning that it is composed of a number of different finer strands of yarn twisted together in the opposite direction to the single plies, giving the finished yarn strength, bounce and durability. Various weights of yarn may be constructed of two, three, six, eight or even more plies.

Tape, ribbon and woven yarns

Modern yarns can vary quite significantly from the traditional spun, plied yarns. One popular variation in yarn structure is the development of various types of woven yarn. These can come in the form of a flat, ribbon-like yarn, tubular, hollow yarns or flattened tubes similar to the construction of a shoelace. Each of these yarns produces a different effect when knitted up and experimentation is the key to success.

Novelty and 'fun fur' yarns

Sometimes known as 'fashion' yarns, these yarn-company offerings are the Marmite of the knitting world. Love them or hate them, most knitters are given a few balls of crazily adorned trimmings from a well-meaning aunt at some point in their knitting history. Whether a knitter can appreciate the aesthetics of a novelty yarn is entirely down to personal preference.

Pocket Tip

Novelty yarns are often suggested as being a good choice for beginner knitters, as the various fluffy extras can hide the odd mistake and dropped stitch, but the same protrusions that hide the mistakes from view can also conspire to hide the stitches on the needles from view and as such can be difficult to knit.

DYEING FOR COLOUR

A number of factors in the dyeing and spinning process can affect the look of a yarn when it has been knitted up. A wide variety of techniques are available to yarn companies and individuals when dyeing yarn, and each technique is capable of producing various effects when turned into fabric.

Solid colours (including natural, un-dyed shades)

Solid colours hold very little surprise and will knit up as expected into a single block of colour.

Semi-solids

Semi-solid colours have slight variations of shade, where either subtly different dyes have been applied or where dye has been allowed to saturate some areas of the hank more than others during the dyeing process. Fabric knitted from semi-solid yarns often has a slightly more 'lively' appearance to it, appearing as if the light is catching the fabric in different areas of the cloth.

Marls

Formed by spinning together two or more plies of differing colours, marled yarns have the appearance of a barber's pole or candy cane. When marled yarns are knitted up they appear to have a flecked, 'snowy' appearance.

Tweeds

Sometimes confused with marled yarns, the defining characteristic of tweed yarn is the inclusion of small 'slubs' of different coloured fibre caught among the twisted plies of yarn. These small inclusions of fibre are in the form of small 'flecks', which appear on the surface of the knitted fabric and give a rustic look to the finished item.

Variegated

Part of the multi-coloured yarn family, variegated yarns are distinguishable by the lengths of the colour repeats. Often beautiful when twisted up into a skein, it can be near impossible to tell how some variegated yarns will appear once knitted into a piece of fabric. Part of the reason for this is a phenomenon known as pooling. When yarn is dyed it is often formed into a loop of approximately 2m in circumference before dye is applied to various sections of this loop. If the pattern repeat causes the required number of stitches to take 2m worth of yarn the individual colours begin to 'line up', causing large blotches (or 'pools') of colour. Some knitters enjoy the thrill of seeing if their latest knitting project will pool, whereas others end up mortified to find that the jumper they have spent weeks knitting has a large fuchsia patch right across the belly.

Pocket Tip

Although pooling is virtually impossible to absolutely prevent, the likelihood of a yarn's instinct to pool can be lessened by alternating two or more balls of yarn, and knitting two or four rows with one ball before knitting a few rows with the alternate skein.

Self-striping

One of the more recent developments in yarn dyeing is self-striping yarns. These yarns have long colour repeats that form bands of colour several rows in height as they are knitted. There are two main types of self-striping yarn: those with abrupt colour changes and those that gradually fade from one hue into another. Striping yarns that change from one colour to another abruptly will form true stripes, though often the colour change will occur in the middle of a row, rather than at the edge. Yarns that slowly transition from one colour to the next will gently fade between colours, giving the knitted fabric the gentle shifting colours reminiscent of a watercolour wash.

Will you stripe or might you pool?

To distinguish a variegated yarn from a self-striping multi-coloured yarn, unwind and examine a strand 2m–3m long, and see how often the yarn changes colour. If the shade changes every 50cm or so it is most likely a variegated yarn, whereas if the length of each colour is a couple of metres or more it will most likely knit into stripes (depending on the width/circumference of the items you are knitting). As might be expected, the longer the stretches of colour, the wider the stripes will be.

Colour-blended

Slow-transitioning self-striping yarn that has been dyed when still in fibre form and then blended whilst spinning is often indistinguishable from self-striping yarn that has been dyed once spun, but usually differs in its less regulated striping pattern and differing width of stripes.

Hand dyed

Yarns created by hand dyeing are usually produced in small quantities and as such it may be hard to find a large number of skeins from the same dye lot. The process often involves laying colours on to a bed of wet yarn and letting them penetrate the yarn. This can lead to irregular colour concentrations, which is the charm of this method. If working with two hand dyed skeins that look to contain different colour mixes, it can be advisable to stripe the two yarns so that the whole garment contains the same mixture of tones and hues.

THE BALL BAND

The label attached to a ball or skein of yarn is known as the ball band. This label gives all the invaluable information a knitter could need to identify the fibre type(s), length and weight of each ball of yarn, and the needle sizes most often associated with that weight of yarn. A diagram outlining the information most often found on a ball band is given below.

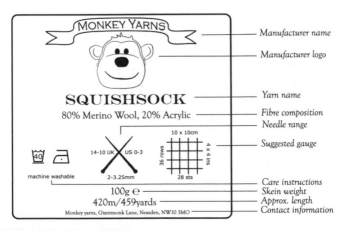

Example of a ball band

FORMS OF YARN

Balls

Most pre-wound balls of yarn can be knitted from the outside of the ball, or the second end can be fished out from inside the ball of yarn to knit from the centre of the ball. Some knitters find this beneficial as it stops the ball from rolling around the floor and getting dirty as it is knitted.

Skein

Other yarn may come in a skein. Skeins look like short, fat sausages of yarn and are usually knitted from the outside. Confusingly, skeins are sometimes referred to as 'balls'.

Hanks

Some manufacturers and independent spinners/dyers package their yarn in hanks. These are long, continuous loops of yarn that need to be wound into a ball by the knitter. Confusingly, hanks are sometimes referred to as 'skeins'.

Yarn companies may choose one way of presenting their yarn over another for aesthetic or storage purposes. Hanks of yarn stack more easily and are less likely to roll off shelves, but it doesn't affect the yarn in any way. The knitter should not worry about the form that the yarn is in unless they have a particular aversion to winding yarn themselves.

Winding a hank of yarn into a ball

It is extremely important to keep the loop stretched over the back of a chair, the knitter's feet or the outstretched arms of a compliant friend whilst wool is wound from a hank into a ball, because if the loop is 'compromised' then an almighty tangle is likely to ensue. Some knitters invest in a 'swift' to minimise the time and inconvenience of winding hanks of yarn into balls. This rotating hank-holder keeps the loop of yarn taught

---

> *as it is wound into a ball. A ball winder is another popular investment for turning hanks of yarn into neatly wound balls, ready to knit in next to no time at all.*

☀ WHERE TO BUY YARN ☀
AND TOOLS

There are many places for the modern knitter to find tools and materials, and the range of items available from different sources is so wide and varied that it can pay to shop around and experience different ways of shopping.

THE YARN STORE

Though the yarn store is not as common a sight as it once was on the high street, many towns still have a yarn store. These may range from a dusty little cove selling mostly acrylic yarns, to Aladdin's caves of bright and jewel-like balls of yarn of all shades and fibres.

DEPARTMENT STORES

Many department stores (such as John Lewis) carry a yarn, fabric and haberdashery department, and these can be wonderful for stocking up on the staple diet of well-known yarn brands. Often carrying the best-known brands and lines, most department stores are well supplied and carry a wide variety of colours in each of their yarns, and often have a good selection of accompanying design-house patterns.

INTERNET SUPPLIERS

Never before have knitters been able to access such a wide variety of yarns. Practically any yarn is available to the needle-wrangler if they are prepared to search for it and pay a little extra shipping if distance dictates. The advantages to buying online can be numerous. Discount yarn bargains and the almost endless variety available are the two main benefits, but what is gained in choice is lost in tactile experience. Internet shopping does not allow the knitter to press the skein of yarn against their cheek or hold it next to their neck to check for the tickle factor. It is impossible to stroll around an internet shop creating colour schemes and comparing shades. Computer monitors vary in how they render colour, so the shade of yarn that arrives can sometimes be markedly different from the shade that the knitter thought that they were getting. There is unfortunately no way around this other than by going to look at the yarn in person. Check a website's terms and conditions before buying to see what their returns policy states, in case the colour that arrives is not the spring green hoped for, but instead the colour of a stagnant pool.

Some websites to visit:

- www.kempswoolshop.com
- www.blacksheepwools.com
- www.texture-yarns.co.uk
- www.cucumberpatch.co.uk

YARN SHOWS AND CRAFT/FARMERS MARKETS

Some of the most interesting yarns can be found on stalls at crafts and farmers' markets, and at yarn shows. Often an outlet for independent ('indie') dyers and spinners, craft stalls can sometimes yield unexpected finds that aren't available in more traditional shops.

ONLINE CRAFT MARKETPLACES

A number of large, international online marketplaces (such as www.etsy.com and www.folksy.com) have been launched in the last few years and many hand spinners and indie dyers use this platform to make their yarns available to the buying public. Some indie dyers may be willing to dye up yarn to a buyer's own specifications too, presenting the opportunity for some truly unique yarn.

DE-STASHES

Knitters love yarn, and sometimes their love can turn into a form of obsession that creeps up on them until one day they are shocked to realise that they have reached the point of SABLE (Stash Acquisition Beyond Life Expectancy), whereby even if they lived to the age of 150 they'd never find enough hours to knit their entire stash. Many of the SABLE breed of knitters reflect upon this moment, shrug, and carry on building their enormous yarn nest regardless, but every now and then a knitter will be shocked enough to de-stash a (small) portion of their collection. It is worth checking on knitting forums from time to time to see if any desperate knitters are hoping for someone to take away part of their yarn mountain for knock-down prices.

SPIN YOUR OWN

Spinning wheels are an investment for the serious spinner, but it is possible to learn to spin with a small amount of equipment costing little (or no) money. A drop spindle is a simple tool that has been used for centuries. Essentially it is a central shaft with a hook on one end and a disc that is used as a weight to keep the spindle spinning and balanced. By setting the spindle rotating whilst slowly feeding in a supply of fibre, a drop-spindle user can spin yarns from fine gossamer-weight lace up to extra-bulky art yarns. Anyone wishing to give drop spindling a go can make a simple drop spindle out of a piece of dowelling (or a chopstick), a small cup hook, a rubber washer and an old CD. Some yarn stores sell pre-dyed fibre for spinning and will often be able to put knitters in touch with local sellers and spinners.

Pocket Fact ☺

Drop spindles have been around for thousands of years, and their design has barely changed in all that time. Images of people using drop spindles can even be seen in the ancient Egyptian pyramids.

THE KNITTER'S TOOL SET

One of the most appealing aspects of knitting is its portability and the relatively few tools and materials a person needs to get started. Needles and yarn are the only two truly essential items for a knitter to begin creating fabric, but knitters tend to like to surround themselves with beautiful and practical items, and as such a knitter's tool kit can hold some wonderful things.

USEFUL ITEMS

The following are some of the most useful items a knitter can possess:

Scissors

Handy for trimming ends and cutting yarn. When a pattern gives the instruction to 'break yarn', it's actually calling for some scissor action.

Stitch markers

Small rings made out of plastic, rubber or metal. These are used to mark sections of knitting – for example, marking where the border of a piece of knitting begins, or where a change of stitch pattern occurs.

Row counter

When knitting a pattern that specifies that a certain number of rows are to be knitted, a row counter can come in very useful. Row counters come in many forms – some fit directly on to the knitting needles, others are designed to be worn around the knitter's neck – but the function is the same. Rotating or clicking the row counter at the end of each row or round the device shows how many rows have been completed to that point.

Pocket Tip

High street hair accessory shops often carry bags of tiny (1cm diameter) rubber hair bands. These brightly coloured, inexpensive rings of rubber make excellent stitch markers. Improvised stitch markers can also be made from tied loops of contrasting yarn in case of a knitting emergency.

Tape measure

A small retractable tape measure is useful for measuring the length of pieces of knitted fabric and can also be used to measure the gauge (see pages 72–73) of the knitted fabric.

Needle gauge

Due to disparities in the systems used to assign sizes to needles of various diameters, a needle gauge can be a handy way of ascertaining the metric measurement of a knitting needle. This handy device is a simple piece of wood, metal or plastic with labelled holes of various diameters drilled into it. Poking a needle into each of the holes until the snuggest fit is found will give an accurate measurement.

Knitter's needle

A knitter's needle is a large, blunt-ended sewing needle, used for weaving in ends after knitting and joining pieces of knitted fabric together to form garments. A large tapestry needle can be substituted for a knitter's needle, but it is important that the one chosen has a blunt, rounded end, so as to not split the strand of yarn when being used.

OPTIONAL EXTRAS

While not absolutely necessary for a knitter's work, these items can no doubt prove useful to own.

Small electronic scale

An electronic scale is useful in determining remaining yarn quantities, especially when calculating if there is enough yarn to complete a project. A good quality kitchen scale that measures in 1g increments will do a good enough job. Pocket-sized jewellery scales will measure even more precisely, in 0.1g increments.

Pins

The magical process of blocking knitted fabric usually requires the liberal use of pins. A lace knitter will often employ 200 pins or more when blocking a moderately sized shawl. It is important to look for rustproof pins, as many blocking techniques use moisture to set the shape of the knitting.

Pocket Fact ☺

The purl stitch had not yet been developed by the fifth century, so all flat knitting was done in the round and then cut to produce flat pieces of fabric. The edges were prevented from fraying using a technique similar to steeking (see Glossary page 166).

Blocking board/mat

Blocking knitted items often requires quite a bit of space. Some knitters choose to block their knitting by pinning it to the carpet, or to the bed (and hoping it dries before night time!) but a dedicated blocking surface might be a good choice for those with little room as it can be propped up against the wall whilst the knitting dries, leaving the floor space clear.

Why it's good to knit

There are a number of benefits to knitting – the most important being that the knitter ends up with loads of gorgeous knitwear – but many knitters also believe knitting has secondary benefits as well, such as being good for combating stress and focusing the mind.

Researchers from Harvard studying the stress-easing benefits of knitting found that knitters can actually lower their heart rate by about 11 beats per minute whilst indulging in their hobby. Brain waves and breathing rate are also slowed during the rhythmic action of knitting.

Some knitters find it a positive way to occupy themselves with forced 'spare time', such as when travelling, feeling that they can accomplish something with those moments waiting in doctor's surgeries or during lunch breaks. Some people also knit whilst watching TV, so that relaxation time can also be productive.

2

GETTING STARTED: BASIC TECHNIQUES

Knitting is not a difficult hobby to master at a basic level. Millions of people have managed to wrangle two needles and a ball of yarn into recognisable, useful and beautiful objects. The important thing to always keep in mind is that mistakes will sometimes happen, but they can be undone and improved upon.

One of the most satisfying things about knitting is that there are really only two stitches: knit and purl. There are many variations of these two basic stitches that twist, manipulate or combine these two building blocks of knitting into more elaborate patterns and forms, but once the knitter is comfortable with the movements of the two fundamental types of stitch everything else is easier to achieve. This chapter will guide you through the basics and help you get started on producing your very own knitted masterpieces.

WAYS OF LEARNING

It is a recognised phenomenon that human beings learn in many different ways, and some ways of learning are more suited to some individuals than others. One knitter may learn best through description and explanation; another may seek the aid of diagrams and pictorial representations. Other knitters benefit from being able to observe another person knitting to mimic the necessary movements; some people may need an even more 'hands on' approach and receive more physical guidance from an experienced knitter.

Pocket Fact ☺

Muscle memory or motor learning is a form of learning physical movements through repetition and familiarity. Typing on a keyboard, playing chords on a guitar and knitting all build muscle memory from subconsciously remembered hand movements.

With the advent of the internet, however, all of these things have become more easily accessible. Instructional videos on sites such as www.youtube.com and www.knittinghelp.com provide detailed explanations and live action video sequences for those in need of more visual help, and finding local knitting groups or knitting classes is only a few clicks away.

Pocket Tip ✄

It's a good idea to keep a small knitting guide (such as the one you are holding now) in your knitting bag at all times in case a new stitch, confusing term or forgotten technique springs up whilst you are knitting.

At first, the process of knitting may seem fiddly and cumbersome, but a little bit of perseverance and practice pays off handsomely as slowly the need to recite the direction of the yarn and where to place the needles drifts to the back of the mind and muscle memory takes over, and the knitter finds that they are happily chatting away to friends over coffee whilst a scarf grows in front of them.

ACCIDENTAL LEARNING AND EXPERIMENTATION

One of the most enjoyable things about knitting is that the small tips and techniques that a knitter picks up along the way can, almost accidentally, grow to become a huge database of knowledge. Looking back on patterns that once seemed impossibly complex can result in the sudden realisation that they later pose no problem to the knitter's newly acquired skills. The emboldened knitter may start to experiment not only with new techniques and patterns, but also with formulating their own designs and modifying existing patterns with new stitch patterns, longer sleeves or a completely different shape, so continuing the knitting adventure.

SOURCES OF HELP AND INSPIRATION

Knitting books and magazines continue to be a source of information, help, patterns and inspiration for knitters, but as the resurgence in popularity of knitting has occurred at the same time as the internet revolution, the two have naturally combined to make the web a fantastic place to turn to for extra help.

Large knitting and crochet community websites, such as www.ravelry.com, can be a fantastic learning resource as many members are very happy to help point newer knitters in the direction of helpful learning materials.

Pocket Fact ☺

The one millionth registered Ravelry user joined the site in 2011.

Magazines and knitting blogs are another fantastic source of inspiration and a way to keep up to date with knitting news and the latest knitwear trends. Personal blogs tend to go into greater detail about the progression of a project than entries on community websites do, so they can be a great resource for finding out how other knitters approach projects and to find solutions to the occasional problem.

KNITTING STYLES

English or Continental? We're not talking about breakfast here, but knitting styles. Just as there is variation in what people choose to eat as their first meal of the day, so there is a difference in how people choose to hold their yarn – the two main recognised styles being known as 'English' and 'Continental'. Happily, neither style of knitting will lead to increased cholesterol, so the knitter is free to just choose whichever they prefer.

Pocket Fact 😀

English style knitting is sometimes known as 'right-handed knitting', while Continental style is sometimes labelled 'left-handed knitting'. These terms can be slightly misleading, as many right-handed knitters knit Continental style and vice versa. The choice is more to do with personal preferences of knitting motion and hand position than whichever happens to be a knitter's dominant hand.

ENGLISH STYLE

Knitters of the English style carry the yarn in the right hand and knit with a motion often known as 'throwing'. When knitting English style, the un-knit working yarn is tensioned around the right hand. Tensioning the yarn is important as it provides a relatively taught short section of the working yarn, which is easier to work with than a very loose and floppy section of yarn. There are many different ways to hold the working yarn and keep it under a comfortable tension. Some knitters wrap a length once or twice around their whole hand, others wrap the yarn around their little finger a couple of times, and still others may run the yarn once around the hand and between the index and middle finger.

When starting to learn how to knit such details may seem cumbersome, and may seem as if the knitter will simply *never* find a comfortable way of holding the yarn. However, once some familiarity with the rhythm of the knitting is established, the knitter will find that they have become accustomed to holding the yarn in a way that is comfortable to them and provides the right amount of tension to knit with – the yarn that is being knitted remains relatively taught but still slips through the fingers or around the hand comfortably, freeing up yarn for the next stitch.

Pocket Tip ✂

Some forms of knitting, such as two-coloured stranded colourwork, can be made by holding one strand of yarn in the right hand,

English style, and a second strand Continental style, in the left hand. Many experienced knitters find it useful to know how to knit in both styles, so even if a knitter is well accustomed to knitting using one particular method it can sometimes be useful to practise the other style from time to time, if only to see if they suddenly find the new style faster, or more comfortable.

CONTINENTAL STYLE

Knitters using the Continental method of holding and tensioning the yarn do so with their left hand. Though it may at first seem that this would be a more difficult style for right-handed knitters this is not necessarily so. A parallel might be drawn with that of a guitar player. The less dominant hand does the tricky work of forming the chords, whilst the dominant hand seems to take on the relatively simple task of strumming the strings. In reality both hands work together in all styles of knitting, just as they do when playing guitar.

The major difference between Continental and English style knitting is that when knitting English style, the yarn is wrapped or thrown around the right-hand needle. When knitting Continental style, however, the needle is used to catch hold of the yarn in an action known as picking, whilst the yarn itself remains in a more or less static position.

Pocket Tip ✂

Many knitters believe that Continental style knitting is a more efficient way of knitting as it requires smaller movements of the hands — due to the yarn being wrapped around the needle using the needle tip itself, rather than by using the hand. The left hand remains static, holding a section of yarn aloft and under tension. New knitters are advised to try both methods and see which one they find most comfortable or natural.

People who have a previous knowledge of crochet may find Continental knitting a good place to start as the yarn is tensioned in the left hand in a very similar manner to how it is tensioned for crochet, and the familiarity of the technique may provide a comfortable transition between the crafts.

Knitting for lefties

There is some disagreement among left-handed knitters as to which is the best way for a left-handed knitter to form knitting stitches.

Some left-handed knitters learn by knitting in an opposite fashion to a right-handed knitter, mirroring the diagrams in knitting books and reversing the actions usually performed with the right hand to perform them with the left. If using this mirrored technique it is important to remember that the written instructions will also need to be reversed, noting that the left needle will now be the right needle, and vice versa, and that wrapping yarn clockwise is to be converted to wrapping it anti-clockwise etc.

Other left-handed knitters find this reversing of knitting instructions both confusing and unnecessary, and knit using the Continental method. As the yarn is tensioned with the left hand when knitting Continental style anyway, many left-handed knitters find this a more natural way to knit. However, as the right-hand needle is used to 'pick' the strand of working yarn, the method may take some getting used to.

As is often the case, the best advice for a new knitter is to try different styles and see which suits them best and remember that most new knitters find the knitting action clumsy at first. If one way leads to frustration, try another, and something may just 'click' into place.

BEGINNING THE KNITTING JOURNEY: THE SLIP KNOT

Even the longest journeys begin with a single step, and with even the most epic of knitting projects that first step is the slip knot. The slip knot provides a single stitch foundation from which the knitting will grow: first horizontally as further stitches are cast on to provide some width for the piece, and then vertically as row after row is added to give the piece of knitting some length.

Making a slip knot

1. *Pull a length of yarn from the ball, about 30cm long.*

2. *Wrap the yarn loosely around the first two fingers of your left hand, forming a loop.*

3. *Pull the yarn attached to the ball between your two wrapped fingers and grasping it there, pull it through the loop.*

4. *Place the newly made loop on to a knitting needle. Pull the tail to tighten and admire the slip knot, which is effectively the first stitch and the first step of a new project.*

THE FORMATION OF THE KNIT STITCH

Once the slip knot has been made, it is useful to consider how it is formed and how it relates to all the other stitches that are going to be knitted. In essence it is very simple – it is a loop of yarn around a needle – but consider a few of the details of that loop.

Hold the needle with the slip knot on it in the left hand and hold the needle horizontally with the point facing right. The loop travels over the needle from front to back. It is important to become accustomed to this little loop of yarn as all knitting stitches are formed this way, with part of the loop facing the knitter and the other part towards the back of the needle. This seemingly small detail can affect the knitting in quite a drastic way, as usually the knitter will be manipulating the front part of this loop, but occasionally, in some more complex stitches, a pattern will direct the needle to knit into the back of this loop, which twists the stitch.

The two sides of a knitting stitch are sometimes known as the front and back 'legs' of a stitch, and a handy visual memento is to imagine the stitch as a little person with legs, sitting astride a log. If the knitting needle is the horizontal log, and the little knitting stitch man is facing left, then the leg nearest the knitter is known as the 'front leg' of the stitch. The part of the stitch that is on the far side of the log is the 'back leg'. Always knit into the front leg of the stitch unless specifically instructed otherwise.

Pocket Tip ✂

Fabric can be made from knitting only into the back leg of the stitch, but instead of forming the balanced and symmetrical 'V'-shaped knitting stitches that most people are used to, it produces fabric in which one half of each stitch forms a vertical column, with the other side of the stitch veering off to one side. This can result in a piece of fabric which biases (skews or twists) and so can be difficult to block and form into well-behaving garments.

🕷 ADDING MORE STITCHES: 🕷 CASTING ON

Once there is one stitch (the slip knot) on the needle, it is time to begin the knitting journey by casting on more stitches. The slip knot counts as a stitch, so if a pattern instructs the knitter to cast on 10 stitches, then nine more are needed to make up the numbers.

Casting on

1. Hold the needle with the slip knot in the left hand (hereafter referred to as the 'left needle') horizontally, with the pointed end facing right.

2. Take the second needle (hereafter referred to as the 'right needle') in the right hand.

3. Taking care to remember how a stitch 'sits' on the needle, insert the tip of the right needle from left to right behind the 'front leg' of the slip knot.

4. Take the yarn anticlockwise around the back of the right needle and bring it forward between the two needles. Hold it out of the way and to the right.

5. Use the left needle to lift the first stitch (the slip knot) over the newly made stitch and off the right needle. Slip the new stitch on the right needle on to the left needle.

6. The left needle now has two stitches cast on and the right needle is free of stitches.

Repeat the above steps, but knitting into the rightmost (last made) cast on stitch each time, adding stitches until the required number of stitches has been made. Remember that the slip knot counts as a stitch in its own right.

The knitted cast on above is a great introductory way to cast on, as the steps used to perform the cast on are all but identical to those used to complete the knit stitch, so once a knitter has accustomed themselves to the knitted cast on they have inadvertently also learned the most important stitch in knitting – the only difference is that when knitting, the old stitch is dropped from the left needle and retained on the right (otherwise the piece of

CAST ON STEP 1

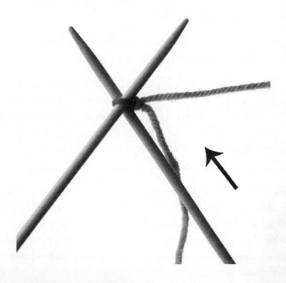

CAST ON STEPS 2 AND 3

CAST ON STEP 4

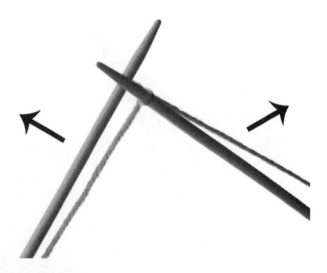

CAST ON STEP 5

CAST ON STEP 5

CAST ON STEP 6

knitting would go on getting wider and wider as new stitches were added!) The alternative cast on method described below is just as effective but doesn't provide the same knit stitch practice.

BACKWARDS LOOP CAST ON

There is an alternative cast on method which you may want to try out to see which method you find easier. Hold the needle with the slip knot on it in your right hand. Holding the length of working yarn in your left hand, run the yarn around the back of your forefinger on your left hand. With the needle in your right hand, pick up the yarn on the left-hand side of the loop sitting round your finger and lift the yarn off your finger and on to the needle. This creates a new stitch. Repeat until you have cast on as many stitches as required.

Pocket Tip

Many people have a tendency to cast on too tightly at first. To help prevent this, many knitters choose a needle size two or three sizes bigger than the one used in the pattern when they cast on, to keep the cast-on edge loose and elastic, rather than firm and unforgiving. Once the stitches have been cast on simply swap back to the required needle size and knit the pattern as directed.

THE KNIT STITCH

Only one stitch is needed to begin knitting – the 'knit' stitch. Once the knitter has successfully learnt the knit stitch they are almost certainly going to want to get comfortable with its reverse side companion, the 'purl' stitch, but almost all new recruits to knitting will start by mastering the humble knit stitch. The knit stitch is the foundation stone of knitting. In fact, the purl stitch is nothing more than the knit stitch in reverse, so it makes sense to begin there.

STOCKINETTE AND GARTER FABRIC

Smooth stockinette fabric that most people would recognise as knitting (rows upon rows of little V-shaped stitches) is formed by knitting one row and purling the next, so that all the 'right' sides of the stitches line up and all the bumpy purl sides of the stitches are kept to the back. However, if you knit every row you will end up with a piece of fabric where each side is composed of alternating rows of smooth 'V's and rows of bumps. This horizontal furrowed fabric is known as garter fabric, and it is the first type of fabric that most knitters attempt because it is so very simple.

FIRST PROJECT

Many books instruct new knitters to knit a garter stitch scarf for their first project as it involves nothing more than casting on a set number of stitches and knitting row after row after row of knit stitches until the scarf is 2m long. This can be problematic though, as many knitters may not get past the first 50cm of their new hobby through sheer boredom.

An alternative project for a knitter's first knitting experiments might be to knit a small (15cm–20cm) square (see page 43 for instructions). This square can be added to using future gauge swatch squares (see Glossary on page 161) and knitting stitch experiments to build up a whole blanket of different coloured and textured pieces, creating an attractive blanket of knitted memories, or simply a memento so the knitter can look back to see how their knitting skills have progressed.

The knit stitch

1. Hold the needle with the row of cast on stitches in the left hand horizontally, with the pointed end facing right.

2. Take the second needle in the right hand and ensure the working yarn is kept at the back of the knitting.

3. Taking care to remember how a stitch 'sits' on the needle, insert the tip of the right needle from left to right (or front to back) behind the front leg of the first (rightmost) stitch on the left needle, making a cross with the needles.

4. Take the yarn anticlockwise around the back of the right needle and bring it forward between the two needles. Hold it out of the way and to the right.

5. The right needle now has a new loop of yarn over it. Slide the right needle down and pull the new loop of yarn on the right needle through the stitch on the left needle. Drop the stitch off the left needle. You have now knitted one stitch, which is on your right needle.

Repeat these steps until you have knitted the entire row of stitches and the left needle is empty. To knit the next row, simply switch the left and right needles so that the empty needle is in the right hand and knit another row. This will form a garter stitch.

KNIT STITCH STEPS 1 TO 3

KNIT STITCH STEP 4

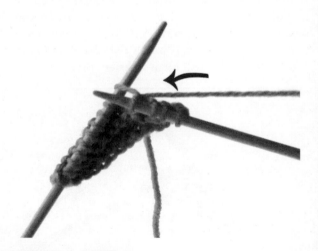

KNIT STITCH STEP 5

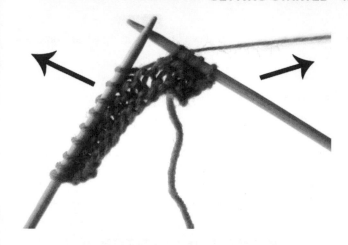

KNIT STITCH STEP 6

✸ COUNTING STITCHES ✸

When learning to knit, it is important to count the stitches after every row. The number of stitches per row should remain constant. One of the most common mistakes made by new knitters is an accidental steady widening of the knitting work as new stitches are inadvertently added whilst knitting. This happens when a knitter brings the working yarn to the front of the piece of knitting between the two needles before making a knit stitch, so creating an increase stitch known as a 'yarn over'. These stitches create a small hole and so are often used in decorative forms of knitting such as lace, where they are paired with decrease stitches to keep the stitch count constant.

The first piece of knitting that a knitter produces will in all likelihood not be perfect, may turn out an odd shape, or have dropped stitches and unexplained holes and twisted sections. New knitters should not be disheartened by this – it is to be expected and is very much how most first knitting attempts start out. Soon the knitter will be accustomed to the anatomy of their knitting stitches and the path that the yarn takes when knitting stitches are being formed – it just takes a little familiarity, which comes with practice.

The first practice square

Using an Aran weight yarn and 5mm needles, cast on 26 stitches. Knit every stitch until one row of knitting has been completed. Turn work, ready to begin another row. Knit until work reaches approximately 15cm long, ready to bind off (see pages 48–52).

✖ THE PURL STITCH ✖

The purl is the companion stitch to the humble knit stitch; its backwards but otherwise identical companion. The knit and purl stitches together form the magic twosome from which pretty much all other stitches and combinations of stitches take their foundations. The purl stitch is needed to create flat pieces of smooth stockinette stitch fabric. Stockinette fabric is the most common type of knitted fabric, and the vast majority of knitted jumpers to be found in the shops are created using this stitch, recognisable by the row upon row of little V-shaped stitches. When a knit stitch is made it forms a little V-stitch at the front of the fabric and a little 'bump' at the back. When the work is turned over and a stitch is knitted, however, the V-shape is now on the 'private' side of the fabric and the bump is showing on the 'public' side (see Glossary, page 165 for more on these terms). The purl stitch allows all of the V-shaped stitches to show from the front of the fabric, however, by essentially making the knit stitch backwards, with the purl bump facing the knitter and the 'V' facing away.

The purl stitch can do more than replicate the knit stitch from behind, however, and forms the basis of much decorative knitting – lending texture and variation to a piece of knitting. Knit and purl

stitches can be combined in an almost countless number of ways
and can be used to add patterning through texture, as in some
forms of traditional Aran knitting. The world is the knitter's oyster
once the purl has been discovered.

The purl stitch

1. Hold the needle with the row of stitches in the left
    hand horizontally, with the pointed end facing right.

2. Take the second needle in the right hand and
    ensure the working yarn is kept at the front of the
    knitting.

3. Taking care to remember how a stitch 'sits' on the
    needle, insert the tip of the right needle from right
    to left (or front to back) behind the front leg of
    the first (rightmost) stitch on the left needle, mak-
    ing a cross with the needles.

4. Take the yarn anticlockwise around from the front
    to the back of the right needle, all the way back to
    the front. Hold it out of the way and to the right.

5. The right needle now has a new loop of yarn over
    it. Slide the right needle down and pull the new
    loop of yarn on the right needle through the stitch
    on the left needle, towards the back. Drop the
    stitch off the left needle. You have now purled one
    stitch, which is on your right needle.

Repeat these steps until you have purled the entire row
of stitches and the left needle is empty.

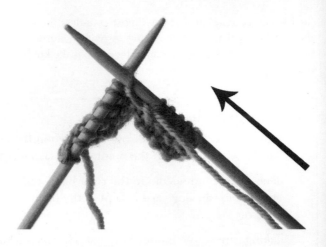

PURL STITCH STEPS 1 TO 3

PURL STITCH STEP 4

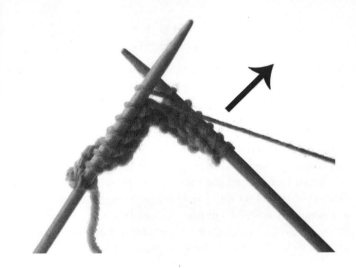

PURL STITCH STEP 5

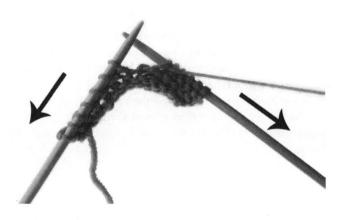

PURL STITCH STEP 6

🕷 HOLDING THE NEEDLES 🕷
AND YARN

Knitting can seem cumbersome at first. Often a new knitter will find it difficult to keep track of their needles, will feel like they need to change their grip with every stitch and will not be comfortable with how they are tensioning the yarn. New knitters should rest assured that they will soon settle into a comfortable way of holding their yarn and needles, and though it may seem like meticulous preparation must go in to remembering how the needles are best grasped and the yarn best tensioned, soon the needles will be picked up with barely a thought as the muscle memory and familiarity with the knitting motions becomes naturally established. The knitter can then move forward in their adventure along the path to knitting excellence by exploring new stitches.

🕷 BINDING OFF 🕷

All good pieces of knitting need to come to an end, and just as casting on is used to establish a first knitting row, so binding off (sometimes known as casting off) is used to provide a secure finishing row.

The simplest bind off is the knitted bind off, which provides an attractive and robust edge to a piece of knitting. A knitted bind off is not very elastic, however, and some knitters have a tendency to bind off too tightly. If the bind-off edge of a piece of knitting pulls inwards and is narrower than the main body of the knitting, some ease can be introduced by using a needle a size or two larger than the main needle size to bind off with, so creating a looser bind-off edge.

The knitted bind off

1. Knit one stitch.

2. Knit another stitch.

3. Using the tip of the left needle, lift the first (right-most) of the two stitches on the right needle over the other and off the needle completely. There should now be only one stitch on the right needle. You have now bound off one stitch.

Repeat steps two and three until only one stitch remains. Cut yarn, leaving a 20cm tail. Use the needle that remains in the last stitch to widen that stitch until the tail of the yarn has been pulled through and off the needle.

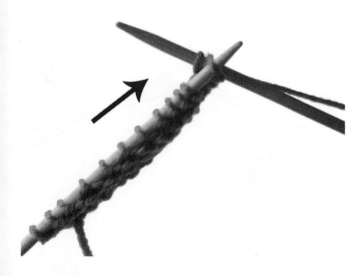

KNITTED BIND OFF STEPS 1 TO 3

KNITTED BIND OFF STEP 3

KNITTED BIND OFF STEP 3

Sometimes a knitter will want a more elastic cast-off edge than a knitted bind off will allow, especially when making items such as socks, where adequate stretch in the cast-off row is essential for both comfort and fit. A good alternative bind off for items where elasticity is needed is the sewn bind off.

The sewn bind off

1. Cut the working yarn, being careful to leave a tail about three times as long as the width of the knitting. Thread this tail of yarn through the eye of a large, blunt-ended tapestry needle.

2. Hold the needle that contains the knitting horizontally in the left hand, with the point facing right.

3. Insert the sewing needle into the first two stitches on the knitting needle from right to left, and draw the yarn through without pulling too tightly.

4. Re-insert the sewing needle into only the first stitch, but this time from left to right, pulling the yarn through again. Drop this stitch off the knitting needle, so binding off one stitch.

Repeat steps 3 and 4 until only one stitch remains. Insert the sewing needle into this stitch from right to left and drop it off the knitting needle.

PATTERNS THAT DON'T REQUIRE BINDING OFF

Not all patterns require binding off. Some items, such as hats, get narrower and narrower as the pattern is knitted, leaving only a few stitches at the crown of the hat. If these were bound off in the traditional manner it would leave a small hole at the very top of the hat. In patterns such as hats and some mittens, there may be an instruction to 'draw the yarn through the remaining stitches'. This instruction is simply carried out by cutting the yarn, leaving a 30cm tail, and threading this tail of yarn through a large, blunt-ended needle. This needle is then passed through all of the remaining stitches on the knitting needle, the knitting needle removed and the yarn tail pulled tight. This pulls all of the remaining stitches together in a circle and closes the hole at the top of the piece of knitting, so ensuring a warm head and a neat finish to the knitting.

🧶 FINISHING 🧶

Once a piece of knitting has been completed, is 'off the needles' and has been admired and appraised, there are usually a few odd jobs that need doing to tidy up and otherwise complete the project. For knitted garments such as cardigans this might involve joining together two or more pieces and sewing on buttons, but for almost all knitting projects this requires the ends being woven in. The tails of yarn from the cast on and bind off rows, and from any instances where a new ball of yarn has been joined in, will need to be woven in to the back of the knitting to both secure them and hide them from view. If they were cut short the cast on and bind off edges would unravel, stitches would run and everything would end in knitting disaster, so remember not to cut the tails too short!

Weaving in ends

1. Thread the tail or 'end' of yarn through the eye of a blunt-ended tapestry needle.

2. With the 'wrong' side of the work facing you, follow a single strand of knitting yarn with the sewing-up needle.

3. Carry on weaving the yarn up and down through the loops across 10 or 12 stitches, checking the front of the work to ensure that the woven yarn tail is not visible.

Cut the end of the yarn and stretch the knitting a little bit, so the yarn tail can work its way around a little. If the end of the yarn works its way to the front after the knitting has been stretched, just poke it back through to the reverse side of the knitting using the point of a knitting needle.

❧ STITCH PATTERNS ❧

Once the purl stitch has been mastered the knitter can begin to experiment with combining the knit and purl stitches together to form other knitting stitches. Many of the most popular and frequently used knitting stitches are formed by combining these two stitches in various patterns, and many stitches can be prac- tised in test squares (similar to the first practice square on page 44), whether just for practice and experience with the aim to gain confidence, or to save for joining together to create a larger-scale project in the future.

Pocket Tip ❧

When working stitch patterns that involve changing between knit and purl stitches on the same row it is important to pay close attention to where the working yarn is before the knit or purl stitch is performed. The working yarn should always be at the back of the work before a knit stitch and the front of the work before a purl stitch. If the working yarn is in the wrong position before knitting a stitch, simply bring it backwards or forwards between the two needles to the correct working position.

STOCKINETTE STITCH

Sometimes known as stocking stitch, stockinette is formed by alternating one row of knit stitches with one row of purl stitches, and produces a smooth simple fabric with a nice balance of drape and give when knitted at a medium tension.

Stockinette has a quirk, in that it curls and rolls. The sides of stockinette curl inwards towards the reverse of the work and a scarf knitted in stockinette will most often resemble a long cylinder rather than a flat rectangle of knitting. Stockinette also rolls vertically, so if used for an item such as a hat the cast on edge will roll up the outside, exposing a roll of reverse stockinette. These qualities can be used for decorative effect in some projects, such as a roll-brimmed hat, but there are many instances in which a knitter will not want any curling of their fabric. Curling isn't an issue for any edges that are joined to another piece of knitting (such as the side seams of a jumper), but other pieces of knitting, such as the open ends of sleeves, will often have another stitch pattern, such as ribbing or moss stitch, which lies flat and keeps rolling at bay.

RIBBING STITCH

There are many versions of ribbing, but all involve forming vertical columns of knit and purl stitches. Ribbing is a very useful and versatile stitch. The vertical furrows formed by the alternative stitches cause the work to contract horizontally, but the work is easily stretched back to full width. This makes ribbing a very elastic stitch and so is perfect for use on cuffs for socks, jumpers and hat brims as it ensures a snug but elastic fit.

The easiest and perhaps most popular ribbing variation is the 1x1 rib, which is a single stitch column of knit stitches followed by single stitch column of purl stitches.

1×1 ribbing

To make 1x1 ribbing, cast on an even number of stitches, then knit one stitch, purl one stitch, and so on until the end of the row – remembering to bring your working yarn to the correct position at the front or back of the work, depending on what stitch is being made. The next row should be knitted in exactly the same way, beginning with a knit stitch, followed by a purl. As an even number of stitches have been cast on, the last stitch of each row is a purl. When the work is turned over this appears as a knit stitch, and knitting this first stitch forms a vertical pattern of knit and purl columns.

2×2 ribbing

A simple variation of ribbing, 2x2 ribbing involves working alternate columns of knit and purl stitches, each two stitches wide. To work 2x2 ribbing, cast on a multiple of four stitches. Knit two stitches, then purl two stitches, until the end of the row. Turn the work and repeat.

Pocket Fact ☺

As 2x2 ribbing contains less switching between knit and purl stitches it is less elastic than 1x1 ribbing. It is the transition between knit and purl stitches that causes ribbing to contract, so the fewer instances of this, the less elastic a ribbing variation will be.

3×1 ribbing

Some variations of ribbing are formed by creating columns of knit and purl stitch that do not match in width. One example of this is 3x1 ribbing, which pairs a three stitch wide column of knit stitches with a purl column that is only a single stitch wide.

To work 3x1 ribbing, cast on a multiple of four stitches. Knit three stitches, then purl one stitch, and repeat until the end of the row and turn work. The second row needs to work the first row in reverse, so knit one stitch, purl three stitches until the end of the row. Repeat these two rows until the work is the desired length.

Other ribbing patterns

By experimenting with various forms of ribbing, a knitter should soon start to recognise what the knit and purl stitches look like from both front and back. Once a knitter is familiar with what knit and purl stitches look like, experimenting with new ribbing patterns becomes very easy as the knitter only has to look at the next stitch to be knitted from the left needle to see if it is a knit or purl stitch. The phrase 'knit the knit stitches and purl the purl stitches' is sometimes used in knitting patterns as a form of short-hand to let the knitter know to look to knit a row of stitches that replicates the row below, simply by looking to see if the next stitch to be knitted has the classic V-shape of a knit stitch or the little 'bump' to show that it is a purl stitch.

Pocket Tip ✄

It is easy to remember that the little 'bump' denotes a purl stitch by thinking of it as a little round 'pearl'.

MOSS STITCH

As easy to knit as 1x1 ribbing, moss stitch involves knitting alternating knit and purl stitches along a row. Unlike ribbing, though, the knits and purls do not line up vertically, but instead are placed one stitch off alignment to form a checkerboard-like pattern. Moss stitch lies flat and will not curl, and so is often used to border other stitches when used for scarves and other patterns that may not otherwise lie flat.

To work moss stitch, cast on an odd number of stitches, and knit one stitch, purl one stitch until the end of the row, ending with a knit stitch. Repeat this row until the desired length has been achieved.

Pocket Fact ☺

Moss stitch is known as seed stitch in American knitting termi-nology. American moss stitch is worked differently to UK moss stitch, involving two-stitch-high columns worked in a checker-board pattern.

SLIPPED STITCHES

Some simple stitch patterns require the use of slipped stitches. Slipping a stitch involves moving a stitch from the left to the right needle without working it. Stitches should always be slipped '*purl-wise*' unless otherwise instructed. To slip a stitch purl-wise, insert the right needle into the stitch on the left-hand needle as if to purl it, but instead of purling the stitch simply move the stitch from the left needle to the right. Slipping a stitch 'knit-wise' involves the same manoeuvre of a stitch from the left to right needle, but instead of inserting the needle into the stitch as if to purl it, insert the needle from right to left, as if to knit it.

COMBINING KNIT AND PURL

There are many other knitting stitches that involve only using the two basic knit and purl stitches to create beautiful textures and effects. Purl stitches on a background of smooth knit stitches can be used to create pictures and symbols, and this technique is often used for knitted cotton washcloths, which make a wonderful quick gift when paired with some handmade or luxury soap.

The 'Holly's Handwarmers' pattern on pages 120–122 is made using only a combination of knit and purl stitches, and the gloves are knitted as a flat rectangle before being joined to create a pair of fingerless gloves with thumb openings. This is a wonderful first pattern for someone who has mastered the knit and purl stitches and wants to try their hand at making something to use and enjoy.

Knitting groups

Knitting can be a fantastic solitary pursuit, but some knitters believe there is nothing better than to gather together to enjoy the expertise and friendly chatter of their knitting friends whilst relishing coffee and cake. A modern take on the knitting circle, knitting groups are held all over the world, and are a great way to learn and share in this ever-growing craft.

Details of local meetings can often be found at local yarn stores or library information points. Alternatively, looking on knitting community forums or using internet search engines could yield some results.

If there is no knitting group in your local area then it might be worthwhile taking the time to set one up. Yarn stores, coffee shops, community centres and pubs are all popular venues for a knitting group (though you should check to see if the proposed pub allows young children if it is intended that knitters should be allowed to bring their children). Good places to publicise knitting groups include yarn stores, library and community notice boards, and knitting community forum websites, especially those that allow regional boards.

Knitting groups usually flourish when they allow for a wide range of skills and expertise, from beginners to those who have been knitting for many years.

3

MAKING THINGS: MORE ADVANCED TECHNIQUES

Learning to knit is an on-going exercise. Once someone has learned to cast on, knit, perhaps purl a little and bind off, they *can* knit. The knitter with basic knowledge can knit squares, and rectangles, and these can be formed into usable and wearable objects, such as scarves, bags and cushion covers, with a little imagination. However, many knitters will want to knit beyond the basic four-sided oblong form and add to their acquired techniques.

MAKING SHAPES

Some patterns, most notably scarves, can be knitted as a long rectangular strip of knitting, with no divergence in width and no corners forming anything other than a comfortable and easy right angle. That would be fine in a world where people only ever wanted to wear and knit scarves, or a land where everyone was composed of boxy shapes and hard, angular flat surfaces.

In the real world, though, people are a lot shapelier, with curves and bumps, and limbs that stick out from the main torso. Most people are going to want to give their knitwear a bit of shape, and for that the knitter needs to know how to increase and decrease the width of their knitting.

INCREASING

To widen a piece of knitting a knitter needs to add more stitches to the rows of knitting that they are working on. There are several ways to increase and each performs a slightly different function and has a slightly different appearance.

Increase stitches are most often worked near the edges of garments so that the piece of knitting lies flat. Some increases can form a decorative line and are used as a design feature on sleeve caps and shoulder/neck areas, while others are designed to be as subtle as possible.

YARN OVER

The most simple of increases is the yarn over. This knitting technique adds a stitch by wrapping the right needle with the working yarn before the next stitch is knitted. The yarn over stitch creates a small hole, which can be used for decorative effect, such as in lace knitting, or even to create a small buttonhole. Yarn over increases are often used when knitting shawls, to create a simple and decorative double row of holes along the 'spine' of the shawl.

Making a yarn over (y/o)

1. Bring the yarn to the front of the work, between the two needles.

2. Hold the yarn to the right, at the back of the right-hand needle, ready for the next stitch.

3. If the next stitch is a knit stitch, knit it. If it is a purl stitch, bring the yarn back to the front, between the two needles, so it is in the correct position for purling.

OTHER INCREASES

Other increases are often used when shaping non-lace garments, when small holes at increase points in the knitting would not be desirable or practical. These other increases come in two main forms: making new stitches between existing stitches, or making two or more stitches from a single stitch. Each have their benefits and can be used decoratively or specifically to blend with the background knitting.

Make one

The 'make one increase' creates a stitch between two existing stitches. It increases slants slightly to the left, which is unnoticeable when the increases are isolated, but can form a decorative slant when placed in a vertical row. The make one increase is also sometimes known as a 'make one left' increase.

How to make one/make one left (M1/M1L)

1. Knit to the point of the increase and hold the tips of the knitting needles apart. There will be a horizontal strand, or 'bar', formed by the previous row of knitting between the two needles. Approaching from the front, use the tip of the left needle to pick up this bar.

2. Insert the right needle from left to right (front to back) through the 'back leg' (see next page) and knit it.

The left-leaning make one increase can be mirrored with a right-leaning make one right increase. Using both forms of increase allows designers to make their knitted pieces symmetrical, so both increases are often used together for best effect.

Make one right (M1R)

1. Knit to the point of the increase and hold the tips of the knitting needles apart. There will be a horizontal strand or 'bar' formed by the previous row of knitting between the two needles. Approaching from the back, use the tip of the left needle to pick up this bar.

2. Insert the right needle from left to right (front to back) through the front leg of this lifted stitch, and knit it as usual.

Both the right-leaning and left-leaning M1 stitches blend in quite well against a background of stockinette stitch, and so make for a good subtle choice when decreases are not intended to be a design feature of the piece.

Pocket Tip

A pattern will usually instruct which increase to use for best effect, but if a pattern calls to 'increase x number of stitches', a 'make one' increase is often the best option as it blends in with a background of stockinette stitch quite seamlessly.

Knit front and back

Another popular increase technique is to knit into the front and back legs of a single stitch, multiple times. Instead of creating a new stitch in a space between two existing stitches, the 'knit front and back increase' works a single stitch a multiple number of times, and can be used to turn a single stitch into two (or more) stitches.

Knitting into the front and back of a single stitch creates a little horizontal 'bar' over the new stitch. This bar is quite invisible in garter stitch but is noticeable when knitting stockinette. Many designers prefer to use a make one increase when designing a pattern in stockinette stitch, but sometimes the horizontal bars of the knit front and back increase can be used for decorative effect, especially when arranged to occur at regular intervals.

Knit front and back (kfb)

1. Using the right needle, knit the stitch as usual, but do not drop the old stitch from the left needle.

2. Manoeuvre the right needle through the back leg of the same stitch, and wrap the yarn around to knit it again.

3. Drop the old stitch off the left needle.

The 'knit front and back' technique can be used to increase one stitch to many stitches by knitting into the front, then back, then front, then stitch as many times as indicated. This may be abbreviated in a similar manner, to kfbfb (or knit front back front back).

By using shaping techniques such as increasing, shapes beyond the regular-sided rectangle become possible. Many triangular shawl patterns make use of simple, regular increases at just four points (one at each side and two in the centre) to create a triangle that starts off only a few stitches wide but ends up with many stitches.

Other triangular shawl patterns start with a greater number of stitches and decrease at regular intervals, until only a few stitches remain. Sometimes there are many ways to achieve a similar shape, and designers may choose one way over another to accommodate a particular design feature, or just out of preference for one technique over another.

Pocket Fact ☺

Worldwide Knit in Public Day is an annual event that takes place on the second Saturday in June each year. The event sees knitters from all over the world take to public places with their needles and yarn, to spread the word that knitting is an enjoyable pursuit for men, women and children of all ages. Visit www.wwkip.com for more information.

DECREASING

Just as a knitter may wish to widen a piece of knitting, so they may wish to make it narrower. Sleeves knitted from the shoulder down require decreasing to allow them to taper towards the wrist. A fitted sweater may require decreasing from the hip to the waist and then increasing back out at the bust, and even simple items like hats require decreasing techniques to form the rounded shape of the crown.

KNIT TWO TOGETHER

Perhaps the simplest and most commonly used decrease (though they are all relatively simple) is the 'knit two together' decrease. The knit two together stitch is a right-leaning decrease and is often found paired with one of a number of left-leaning decreases when used to make a symmetrical garment.

Knit two together (k2tog)

1. Insert the tip of the right needle from left to right (front to back) behind the 'front' legs of the first (rightmost) two stitches on the left needle – first through the left of these two stitches, then through the right.

2. Knit these two stitches as if they were a single stitch, drawing a single loop of yarn through the two stitches.

Though the knit two together stitch is easily the most common right-slanting decrease, left-slanting decreases are less predictable. Some designers prefer one choice over the others through either ease of performing the stitch or for aesthetic purposes. Often these decreases are interchangeable, so if the knitter finds that they prefer the look or action of one left-leaning decrease over the others they can usually swap the decrease method for the one of choice without disrupting the knitting.

SLIP, SLIP, KNIT

One of the most popular left-leaning decreases is the slip, slip, knit, which mirrors the knit two together stitch quite closely.

Slip, slip, knit (SSK)

1. Insert the tip of the right needle into the first stitch as if to knit it, but instead of knitting it let it drop off the left needle, transferring it to the right needle. This is known as slipping the stitch 'knit-wise'.

2. Do the same with the next stitch.

3. Insert left needle into the front loops of the slipped stitches (from left to right) and knit them together through the back loops.

Some knitters prefer to work the slip, slip, knit decrease slightly differently, by slipping the first stitch as described in step one, but slipping the second stitch by inserting the right needle as if to purl and transferring the stitch from left to right needle in this way. It simply a matter of personal preference how the knitter performs the slip, slip, knit decrease, though some people believe that the second way helps the decrease to lie a little flatter and so find it more attractive.

SLIP, KNIT, PASS

Another left-leaning decrease involves slipping a stitch to later pass over another stitch, in an action similar to a knitted bind off. Known as a slip, knit, pass (or sometimes as slip one, knit one, pass slipped stitch over) decrease, the resulting stitch is the same as the slip, slip stitch, albeit performed in a rather different way.

Slip one, knit one, pass slipped stitch over (SKP)

1. Insert the tip of the right needle into the first stitch as if to knit it, but instead of knitting it let it drop off the left needle, transferring it to the right needle.

2. Knit the next stitch.

3. Using the tip of the left needle, lift the slipped stitch over the knitted stitch and drop it off the right needle.

A good exercise for practising increases and decreases is to start with a piece of knitting 20 stitches wide. Knit one stitch and then make a right-leaning decrease. Knit until three stitches before the end of the row and then make a left-leaning decrease. Purl the reverse row before repeating the exercise. Do this until there are only six stitches left. Next, on the right side row, practise doing right- and left-leaning increases, leaving one stitch either side of the increase spot. This will result in a piece of knitting that narrows and then widens again, and gives the knitter a good opportunity to try out various increases and decreases to see how they function and which they prefer the look of. The resulting piece of knitting can be labelled with the various increases and decreases use and kept for future reference.

✸ ADDING A NEW DIMENSION: ✸ KNITTING IN THE ROUND

In a world where knitting is flat but the people wearing the items have a lot more depth to them, pieces of knitting need to be joined together to fit around the three-dimensional shapes of which the body is composed. But knitting doesn't have to be flat, because of the existence of a technique known as 'knitting in the round'.

CIRCULAR NEEDLES

Knitting in the round is usually done using a special type of needle called a circular needle. A circular needle comprises two short needle tips joined by a smooth flexible cable. Stitches are cast on to this needle before the two ends of the cast on row are joined to create a circle, which is then added to by knitting round and round to form a tube of fabric, which is essentially knitted in a very long spiral.

Pocket Tip ✄

Circular knitting is especially quick to work when knitting stockinette stitch. As knitting in the round involves knitting in a circle with the right side always facing the knitter, there is never any need to purl.

Cylindrical knits are perfect for producing smooth, comfortable fabrics where seams would be bulky, restrictive or otherwise uncomfortable – such as when making socks or mittens.

Knitting in the round

1. Cast on the required number of stitches using the circular needle.

2. Hold the needle tip that has the working yarn coming from it in the right hand.

3. Make sure that all of the stitches on the circular needle are facing the same way, with the loops ready to knit at the top, and the cast on end at the bottom. Hold the second needle tip in the left hand.

4. Place a stitch marker on the tip of the right-hand needle to mark the beginning of the round.

5. Knit the first stitch from the left needle, and continue knitting according to the pattern directions.

It is important to make sure that all stitches are properly aligned before joining to knit in the round, otherwise the cast on edge will be twisted. If the cast on edge does become twisted, the only solution is to undo the knitting and start again.

Circular needles come in a wide variety of lengths, from long needles over 1m in length (used when knitting the torsos of jumpers and other items which require a large number of stitches to be on the needles), to small 20cm diameter needles (used for making small-diameter items such as socks). Such small-diameter circular knitting needles are a fairly recent product on the market, and are only one of a few different ways to knit small-diameter cylinders of fabric.

DOUBLE POINTED NEEDLES (DPNS)

Another popular method of small-diameter knitting uses a set of short needles with points at each end, known as double pointed needles, often abbreviated to DPNs.

Pocket Fact ☺

DPNs are not a recent invention, and knitting in the round has been an established technique for many hundreds of years. There was a fashion in the 14th century for paintings that depicted the Madonna engaged in a spot of knitting. The Madonna is almost always shown to be knitting in the round using DPNs.

Double pointed needles are usually sold in sets of four or five short needles. When using DPNs, stitches are cast on and distributed between all but one of the needles in the set, and the three or four needles containing the cast on stitches are arranged in a triangle or square so the first and last needles are made to meet, ready to be joined to knit in the round. The one remaining needle free of stitches is then used to knit from the first needle, freeing that needle of stitches. The new free needle is then used to knit all of the stitches from the next needle, and so on, until a full round has been completed.

Some new knitters find DPNs fiddly to begin with, but other knitters find DPNs to be their preferred method for knitting in the round due to portability, comfort or personal preference. It is worth experimenting with different methods of small-diameter knitting, especially if knitting socks, as many people find that they vastly prefer one method over another.

Pocket Fact ☺

An attempt to make the world's largest hand-knitted sock began in the UK in 2006 as part of the Big Sock event. The sock is 1,500 stitches in diameter so far and is travelling around the world, being added to by the efforts of hundreds of knitters, ranging in age from four to over 80.

MAGIC LOOPING

Another method of knitting small-diameter pieces is known as Magic Looping. Magic Loop knitting is performed on a circular needle, but one much larger than the actual diameter of the item being knitted (a good rule of thumb is to use a circular needle that is at least four times the diameter of the item being knitted). Magic Loop knitting requires the additional length of the circular needle's cable to emerge between stitches, so it is important to use a circular needle with a very fine and flexible cable when using this method.

Magic Looping

1. Cast on the required number of stitches needed for the pattern.

2. Slide all of the cast on stitches down on to the flexible cable part of the circular needle.

3. Pick a point half way along the row of cast on stitches and part two of the stitches, grasping the cable of the circular needle. Gently bend this cable and pull until the looped section of cable emerges from between the two groups of stitches.

4. Slide the two groups of stitches down on to the needle tips. Half of the total number of stitches should be on each needle tip. Hold the needles so that the working yarn is hanging from the back needle and ensure the cast on stitches are not twisted.

5. Holding the front needle with the left hand, slide the stitches of the back needle down on to the cable part of the circular needle, freeing the front needle tip. Hold this needle tip in the right hand.

6. Knit all the stitches from the left needle using the empty needle tip. Half a round has now been knitted.

7. Turn the circular needle so that both needle tips are now pointing to the right.

8. Slide the stitches on the cable on to the new front needle tip.

Repeating steps 5–8 completes one full round. Continue in this manner, knitting half a round at a time.

Redistributing the stitches along the needle tips and cable in order to knit using the Magic Loop method may seem time consuming and taxing at first, but many knitters soon find that the method becomes lot quicker once they have knitted a few rounds, and confidence in remembering which stitches are to be redistributed to which needle becomes second nature.

ADVANTAGES AND DISADVANTAGES

Each method of small-diameter knitting has its benefits and its drawbacks. Small-diameter circular needles can be difficult to source (though they are becoming more readily available from online merchants) and some people find the very short needles tips fiddly, but they are very portable and require no redistributing of stitches.

DPNs are similarly portable but have longer needle tips to grasp, meaning some knitters worry that stitches might inadvertently slide off the unguarded needle ends whilst knitting or when transporting their current knitting project.

Magic Looping provides the security of a longer needle but requires a bit more room to perform than either of the other two methods, due to the necessary redistribution of stitches, so is perhaps less handy for the hassled commuter. The key is usually to try all of the available methods and see which feels the most comfortable and which gives the best results.

SWATCH, SWATCH, SWATCH

Knitters often find themselves asking:

- 'Will a jumper look right if knitted in a larger size but at a finer gauge?'

- 'Will substituting a smooth cotton yarn with a fluffy mohair yarn affect the drape of the garment?'

- 'Will knitting an intricate cable pattern in a bouclé yarn affect the definition of the cables?'

- 'Will changing up a single needle size *really* make much difference to the size of the finished item?'

These questions can all be answered by the simple answer: swatch, swatch, swatch. Knitters need to swatch, and measure. Then wash, block and measure again.

Pocket Tip

It is important to create a swatch or gauge before embarking on any project, because the swatch determines whether the pattern is going to knit to the right tension. Put simply, the tension swatch aims to make sure that the knitter's stitches are the right size before many hours of knitting are put into knitting a jumper that would look massive even on the average darts player.

A knitted swatch is simply a small 15cm–20cm square of knitting, knitted in the same stitch pattern as the intended garment, which is then measured to check how many stitches and how many rows the knitter is getting for every 10cm of fabric. Hopefully the answer will be the same as that specified by the pattern, but if the knitter is getting too many stitches per 10cm then a larger needle should be selected and another swatch knitted. If too few stitches are counted for every 10cm then a smaller needle should be tried.

KNITTING A GAUGE SWATCH

To knit a gauge swatch, cast on the number of stitches that the pattern suggests knitters should be getting per 10cm, plus half that number again. Knit in the specified stitch pattern until the gauge swatch is 15cm long, and bind off loosely. Wash and block the swatch without stretching the knitting, and then pin to dry. When the knitting has dried use two dressmaker's pins to mark a horizontal row of knitting 10cm wide. Count the number of stitches between the two pins and make a note of the resulting number. Repeat this two or three more times, and take the average of these numbers.

Repeat the measuring again, but this time marking a 10cm vertical column of stitches, and measure to determine the row gauge.

Pocket Tip ✄

When knitting small items, such as the Holly's Handwarmers pattern on pages 120–122, the finished item is not much bigger than the gauge swatch would be. In these instances the knitter may find it preferable to just begin knitting the pattern with the suggested needle size and to measure the gauge at various points along the way, as taking a gauge swatch may take just as much time as it would to knit the finished item. If it transpires that the gauge isn't correct, there is no more work lost in beginning the small project again as there would be in undoing the gauge swatch.

After a gauge swatch has been knitted and the correct gauge has been determined, the swatch can be unravelled and the freed yarn used for the project being knitted. Alternatively, swatches can be kept as part of a knitting file or to be joined together into a patchwork swatch cushion or baby blanket.

🪲 THE MAGIC OF BLOCKING 🪲

Many knitters would not hesitate to describe the process of blocking as magical. Proving that it *is* possible to make a silk purse out of a sow's ear, blocking has the ability to take a lumpy, uneven piece of misshapen knitting and whip it into shape. Blocking is knitting's equivalent of a shampoo and set, using water or steam to 'set' stitches into a uniform and pleasing formation. Wet-blocking also provides a good opportunity to give the finished item a freshen-up before wear.

Pocket Fact ☺

Blocking can work wonders on all types of knitting, but nowhere do the amazing properties of blocking shine more than when used with lace knitting. All of the small, decorative holes that form the lace pattern are pulled into shape and a piece of lace can grow to nearly twice the unblocked size, providing great satisfaction at the size of the finished knitted piece.

Blocking requires a little time, patience and space, but gives a professional finish to garments and as such is worth the extra effort. Most natural fibres can be blocked, but man-made fibres such as acrylic are less susceptible to its powers.

WET BLOCKING

To wet block wool and other natural fibres, first wash the knitted pieces as directed by the care instructions on the yarn label. Place the wet pieces between layers of towels and stand on the towels to remove most of the water. Following the pattern schematic (see page 95), pin out the pieces to the specified dimensions, using a blocking board and rustproof pins. An extra couple of inches can be added to a sweater this way, which can be useful if the required size has changed between the date the item was cast on and when it was finally off the needles.

Leave the pieces to dry fully, before unpinning, ready to be seamed or worn.

STEAM BLOCKING

Many people prefer steam blocking as an alternative method to wet blocking as it is faster and requires little drying time. Steam-blocking should always be tested on a knitted swatch before committing the entire garment to this hot treatment though.

To steam block an item, make sure the knitting is pinned to the required dimensions on a heat-proof surface such as an ironing board. Using an iron with a steam setting, hold the jet of steam 30cm from the surface of the knitting and give the item an all over blast of steam. Leave to fully cool and dry before unpinning.

Pocket Tip

Blocking boards can be an expensive outlay if they are only for occasional use. Many knitters pin their blocking items to a spare bed covered in plastic, or even to the carpet, but this requires sacrificing space for the sake of beautiful knitwear. An inexpensive alternative to a purpose-made blocking board is to buy a set of cheap interlocking foam tiles, intended for children's play areas. These can be found in many toy stores and supermarkets, split into individual tiles for easy storage and can be joined together in many formations to block items of many shapes. They can be propped against a spare wall whilst items are drying, so saving valuable floor space and allowing the knitter to retain their bed sleep soundly, dreaming of yarn.

BLOCKING ACRYLIC

Many knitters will claim that acrylic absolutely cannot be blocked, but it is worth remembering that not all acrylic yarns are created equally, and soft, modern acrylics are a far cry from the rough and squeaky acrylics manufactured in the 1970s. Some knitters find there is noticeable benefit in steam-blocking acrylic yarn, allowing knitted pieces to lie flat and the edges to remain straight. At the very least it may be worth the knitter experimenting with steam block-ing acrylic pieces to see for themselves if it makes a difference.

Killing acrylic yarn

There is a form of heat-processing acrylic yarn known as 'killing'. To kill acrylic yarn involves subjecting the item to short periods of high heat. This changes the nature of the yarn completely, giving the item greater lustre and drape. Killing acrylic is a one-way street and cannot be undone, so should always be practised on a test swatch before committing the entire piece to the iron.

To kill acrylic, dampen the item and pin it to the desired proportions on a damp towel. Place another damp towel on top of the item and place a hot iron on top for five seconds. Move the iron to a new position and repeat. Leave the item to cool and dry before unpinning.

🐝 PUTTING ALL THE PIECES 🐝 TOGETHER

Once all the pieces have been knitted and blocked, there is only one step between the knitter and the completion of their amazing creation: joining all of the pieces together. Pieces can be joined before the item is blocked, but blocking makes the process of sewing-up far easier, and as such, more pleasurable. The edges of a blocked piece of knitting are more clearly defined and as such the stitches are more distinct. If tails of yarn have been left after knitting, these can be used for seaming up. Otherwise, a tapestry needle should be threaded with a new piece of yarn, ready to begin the join.

There are several methods of sewing up an item, and each has its particular uses and applications. Some patterns will specify which method to use when sewing up a garment, but others will leave it to the knitter's judgement and experience. If in doubt, the knitter can always knit a couple of small swatches and try a few different methods to see how they perform with that particular edge and yarn.

MATTRESS STITCH

One of the most often used joining techniques is the mattress stitch. This is the preferred joining method for many knitters, as it results in an invisible join and the appearance of a smooth, continuous piece of fabric.

Mattress stitching a vertical seam

1. With the right sides of the two pieces of knitting facing the knitter and placed side by side as they are going to be joined, bring the threaded needle up from back to front, through the very bottom corner stitch of the left piece of knitting.

2. Bring the needle up through the bottom corner of the right piece in the same manner.

---

3. Stretch the bottom of the left-hand piece of knitting slightly, to ease the very first stitch to the right, exposing the little 'bars' that lie between the stitches. Insert the sewing needle from bottom to top under the bottom two bars on the left piece. Pull the yarn through but do not pull it tight – leave about 2cm of slack yarn.

4. Do the same with the right-hand piece of knitting, sliding the needle from bottom to top under the lowest two bars between the first and second stitches. Pull the yarn through, leaving 2cm of slack.

5. Take the needle back to the left-hand piece of knitting. This time, take the needle under the third and fourth bars between the first and second stitches.

6. Repeat this on the right-hand piece of knitting.

Carry on in this manner, always leaving 2cm of slack yarn, until you run out of yarn or the top of the pieces of knitting has been reached. Starting at the bottom, slowly and gently pull each piece of slack yarn to ease the two sides together, as if tying the laces on a shoe. Do not pull the slack yarn too tightly – the intention is to ease the sides together without distorting the adjacent stitches. When all the slack has been taken up, use the tail of yarn to carry on seaming or to weave in and finish.

Mattress stitching leaves a one-stitch-deep seam on the inside of the garment, which is invisible on the public side. In some garments a side seam can lend some stability to the knitting and can help prevent twisting of the garment around the torso. In very fine knit garments, though, this seam can feel quite substantial, so a side-to-side seam is sometimes preferred.

SIDE-TO-SIDE SEAM

The side-to-side seam (also sometimes known as an edge-to-edge seam) is worked with the reverse sides of the garment facing the knitter. When worked on garter stitch items it can look almost invisible, but leaves a noticeable line of stitching on stockinette items.

Side-to-side seaming

1. Start with both pieces of knitting laid side-by-side with the wrong sides showing.

2. Beginning at the bottom, bring the needle up through the very edge stitch on the left piece of knitting, leaving 2cm of slack yarn.

3. Bring the needle up through the leftmost bump on the right-hand piece of fabric, leaving 2cm of slack yarn.

4. Bring the needle up through the second-from-bottom bump on the left piece of knitting in the same manner.

Carry on working this way, first sewing through the left and then the right pieces of fabric, moving up one row at a time. When the entire seam has been completed, ease the two pieces of knitting together by taking up the slack yarn between them – being careful not to distort the stitches by tightening too much.

Both the mattress stitch and side-to-side seaming techniques provide a good amount of vertical ease to accompany the natural stretch of the knitted fabric. There are times, however, when a designer intends for a sturdier seam that will resist stretching, perhaps to counteract the heaviness of a piece of fabric, or to provide structure to a knitted bag. In these cases, backstitching may be used as a far less stretchy seam.

BACKSTITCHING

Backstitching can be used for both vertical and horizontal joins, and is sometimes used for shoulder seams to prevent the seam from stretching under the weight of the sleeve.

Backstitch

1. Place both pieces of fabric together, with the right sides facing and the edges to be joined at the top.

2. Working about half a centimetre from the top edge, bring the needle through both pieces of fabric from back to front, between the first and second stitches.

3. Take the needle from front to back, at the very rightmost edge of the two pieces of fabric.

4. Bring the needle through both pieces of fabric from back to front, between the second and third stitches.

5. Next, take the needle from front to back, between the first and second stitches.

Carry on in this manner, working from right to left, until all stitches have been sewn and the seam is complete. Being sure to bring the needle through at the same spot on both pieces of fabric will ensure a neat join.

Whichever method is used, seaming pieces of fabric requires the pieces of fabric that are joined to be bound off before joining. However, there are some instances where a knitter will want to join two pieces of knitting that still have live stitches – whether it be two sets of stitches still on the needles, one set still on the needles and one on a stitch holder, or when joining two sides of a tube of knitting together to provide a closed end. Other techniques can be used for making these kinds of joins, and they are really quite ingenious.

JOINING LIVE STITCHES

Sometimes a knitter wants to join two pieces of knitting without binding off first. One example of this would be when knitting the toe of a sock. The humble sock is basically a tube with a kink in the middle, which is closed at one end. When closing that end, the knitter could bind off all the stitches of the tube and then sew the tube shut. This would work just fine, but the result would not be very pleasurable to wear. Anyone with unpleasant memories of badly made socks with a rough, bulky seam irritating their toes can attest to this. Another option is to use the Kitchener stitch.

Kitchener stitch

A smooth join without added bulk is less likely to catch on toe-nails and is far more pleasurable to wear, and thus the Kitchener stitch arrives on the scene like a crime-fighting superhero, ready to rid the world of the scourge of uncomfortable sock toes.

Pocket Fact ☺

The Kitchener stitch is named after Lord Kitchener (he of the 'Your Country Needs YOU' posters from the First World War.) Kitchener was behind the efforts to encourage women to knit for those people serving abroad, and the items in most demand were socks. At the time the toes of socks were bound off and then seamed, and would cause irritation to the feet of men who were expected to walk many miles every day. It is believed that Lord Kitchener was behind the drive to find a way of producing a completely smooth join to form a comfortable end to a pair of socks.

HOLLY'S HANDWARMERS (PAGE 120)

HOLLY'S HANDWARMERS (PAGE 120)

GREENWOOD HAT (PAGE 123)

WINTER CUDDLES HOT WATER BOTTLE
COVER (PAGE 127)

WINTER CUDDLES HOT WATER BOTTLE
COVER (PAGE 127)

VIVIANNE SCARF (PAGE 132)

BANDY LEGS SOCKS (PAGE 134)

The reason that the Kitchener stitch is so very smooth is because the join itself has exactly the same structure as a single row of knitting, so using this technique results in a completely invisible join that is part of the knitted fabric.

When joining two separate pieces of fabric using the Kitchener stitch, they should be of equal stitch counts and placed, ready to work, with the wrong sides facing. When joining a tube of knitting, such as the toe of the sock, the tube should be folded in half with the right side out and the two sets of stitches placed on separate needles.

Kitchener stitch

1. Place the two sets of live stitches with the wrong sides inwards and both needle points facing right. The needle closest to the knitter is the 'front' needle, and the other is the 'back' needle.

2. Pass the blunt-ended sewing-up needle and a length of yarn from right to left through the first stitch on the front needle, leaving the stitch on the needle. Leave 1cm of slack yarn.

3. Pass the sewing needle from left to right through the first stitch on the back needle, leaving the stitch on the needle. Leave a little slack yarn after each stitch.

4. Pass the needle from left to right through the first stitch on the front needle, then drop that stitch from the knitting needle.

5. Pass the sewing needle from right to left through the next stitch on the front needle, this time leaving the stitch on the knitting needle.

6. Pass the sewing needle from right to left through the first stitch on the back needle, and drop this stitch from the knitting needle.

7. Pass the sewing needle from left to right through the next stitch on the back needle, this time leaving the stitch in place.

8. Repeat steps 4–7 until only one stitch remains on each needle, then repeat step 4 followed by step 6.

Three-needle bind off

Another way of joining two sets of live stitches is known as a three-needle bind off. This technique should perhaps be known as a three-needle bind off and join, as it forms a join between two pieces of fabric whilst also being worked rather like a knitted bind off.

Unlike the Kitchener stitch, the three-needle bind off is worked with the right sides of the two pieces of knitting facing each other. This bind off creates a sturdy, if somewhat bulky, join in relation to Kitchener stitching, but is useful for areas such as shoulder seams and the bases of bags and purses.

Three-needle bind off

1. To work the three-needle bind off, hold the two pieces of fabric together with the right sides touching.

2. The needles in the two sets of stitches should both have their tips pointing towards the right. They will both act as the left-hand needle, so should be held together as one needle, in the left hand.

3. Using a third needle, knit the first stitches of the front and back needle together, dropping both stitches from their left needles. Do this by inserting the right needle through the front of the first stitch of the first needle, then the first stitch of the

back needle. Wrap the working yarn around the right needle as usual and draw that loop through both left needle stitches.

4. Repeat this action with the next stitches on the left-hand needle. Use the tip of one of the left-hand needles to lift the first stitch over the second and off the right-hand needle, as in a standard knitted bind off.

So, there are ways of joining two bound off pieces of fabric, and ways of joining two sets of live stitches. But, what if the knitter wants to take a bound off piece of knitting and make some live stitches appear along one of its edges? Then it's time to pick up stitches.

🐝 PICKING UP STITCHES 🐝

Why would a knitter want to pick up stitches that they haven't dropped? This isn't the same technique as rescuing escapee knits and purls, though the names are similar (see Chapter 7 for how to rescue stitches). Sometimes known as the pick up and knit (or purl) technique, this skill allows the knitter to establish a row of stitches to join a new piece of fabric to one that has already been knitted. This technique is used to join the main body of the hat to the sideways knitted brim in the Greenwood Hat pattern on pages 123–126, and, as demonstrated in that pattern, is fantastic for joining one piece of knitting perpendicular to another piece of knitting.

Pick up and knit

1. Starting at the right-hand side of the knitting with the correct side facing the knitter, put the tip of the knitting needle through a stitch near the top of the piece of knitting.

2. Wrap the working yarn as if knitting, and pull through a loop. One stitch is picked up.

3. Moving to the left and keeping in line with the first picked up stitch, repeat this action until the required number of stitches has been picked up.

Some knitters dislike picking up stitches, finding it fiddly and time consuming, but the action is little different from the standard knitting action. If, however, the knitter does find it difficult to pick up the stitches easily, it is possible to cheat a little with the deft use of a crochet hook. Starting at the right-hand side of the fabric, simply insert the crochet hook from front to back and draw through a loop of working yarn, then place this loop on to a waiting knitting needle. Repeat as many times as required.

PICK UP AND PURL

A less-often-seen instruction is the 'pick up and purl' command. Worked similarly to the first technique, the needle (or crochet hook) should this time be inserted from the back of the piece of fabric and the yarn wrapped purl-wise, before drawing the loop of working yarn through to the back.

✂ MODIFICATIONS ✂

As a knitter comes to a greater understanding, through practice, of how a garment is constructed and how certain stitches affect the drape and look of the fabric, they may start to wish they could make a few changes to published patterns to give them a different neckline, or to change the length or stitch pattern.

Personal modifications can give additional style to a knitted item, and once the fundamentals of shaping and fit are understood, garments can be tweaked to be more flattering and individual. A modification as small as altering the sleeve length on a sweater can give a whole new style and function to the finished piece, and changing the stitch pattern can take a plain knit cardigan into a piece of evening wear full of charming detail. The best thing to do is experiment and see where modifications lead.

✄ KNITTING TRADITIONS ✄

Many knitting traditions specific to certain areas, their people and cultures, are still popular today. Such knitting traditions are often defined by the geographic area where they developed and so carry the name of that place.

ARAN KNITTING

The Aran Islands lie off the West Coast of Ireland and lend their name to a particular type of textured knitting, traditionally used for fisherman's thick sweaters. Traditional Aran sweaters were made from natural, un-dyed cream-coloured wool. The wool was often untreated and still contained lanolin, which gave the knitwear some degree of waterproofing, making it particularly useful for work at sea.

Some of the traditional stitch motifs found on Aran sweaters may have symbolic significance. The honeycomb pattern is said to represent the industriousness of the bee, and twisted rope-like cables represent part of every fisherman's daily routine in the hauling in of ropes and nets.

Pocket Fact ☺

A popular and oft-repeated myth claims that Aran sweaters were knitted with family-specific patterning, so that if a sailor were to fall overboard and drown his body (should it wash up or be recovered some time later) would be easily identifiable by the motifs on his knitwear. There is no historical evidence for this idea though, and the belief may have instead stemmed from a 1904 play by J. M. Synge called Riders to the Sea. *In the play a fisherman's body washes up on the shore and is identified by his hand-crafted knitwear.*

FAIR ISLE

Among Scotland's Shetland Islands lies the tiny area of land that is the Fair Isle: home to only 70 residents. This area lends its name to a particular form of stranded colourwork, incorporating motifs traditional to the area which sit in horizontal bands of colour. Many people use the term 'Fair Isle' to refer to any form of stranded colourwork, whereas traditionalists prefer to use the term only for the very specific patterning traditional to the area.

Fair Isle sweaters became high fashion in the 1920s, when the stylish then Prince of Wales (later to ascend the throne as Edward VIII) was photographed wearing a variety of highly patterned Fair Isle tank tops.

Pocket Fact ☺

The year 2010 saw discussions as to whether or not 'Fair Isle' should become a protected term in the same way that Harris Tweed and Champagne are. If successful, Fair Isle-style sweaters produced in other areas of the UK or the rest of the world would be banned from using the term 'Fair Isle' to market their goods. There is some disagreement whether the protected term 'Fair Isle' should be applied to garments created in the whole of the Shetland Islands or for garments created on Fair Isle alone, where just 70 people reside — only four of whom can knit.

NORWEGIAN COLOURWORK

Another form of stranded colourwork can be found in the Norwegian knitting tradition. Selbu knitting often features traditional snowflake and star-shaped motifs and other traditional patterning. Unlike Fair Isle knitting, Norwegian colourwork usually has a restrictive palette of two colours, often black and white, giving it a high-contrast visual aesthetic.

ESTONIAN LACE

One of the most intricate lace traditions has its origins in Estonia. The most prominent feature in Estonian lace is the combination of openwork and texture stitches. One of the most popular ways of adding texture in Estonian lace is the making of nupps. A nupp is a small bobble resembling a flower bud. These are created by increasing one stitch through a series of knits and yarn-overs until it becomes five, seven, nine or even 11 stitches, and then purling all of these stitches together on the return row.

ICELANDIC LOPI KNITTING

Though the cold and harsh winters of Iceland have meant that the country has a long tradition of knitting, the Icelandic Lopi form of knitting was not developed until the early part of the 20th century, when knitters began to experiment with knitting barely twisted *roving* rather than pre-spun yarn. The resulting warm, thick sweaters soon became very popular, and the patterned round-yoked jumpers often made with this technique remain popular today.

READING PATTERNS
AND PICKING PROJECTS

Knitters mostly rely on tried and tested knitting patterns when deciding what to knit. The advent of the internet has seen a surge of sources from which a knitter may find knitting patterns, from classic and vintage knits to avant-garde, barely wearable art pieces. Never before have knitting patterns been so accessible or so varied, but most share a common structure of presentation which has become the accepted form when presenting a set of knitting instructions. This chapter reveals how to read these instructions and also includes some tips for finding and choosing patterns.

✿ HOW TO READ A PATTERN ✿

A knitting pattern can seem like a daunting amount of information to try and take in at first, but as long as the information is approached in a methodical way it soon becomes very easy to 'read' a pattern. Most knitting patterns will contain a number of sections, each one dealing with an element that will help to make the finished project a success.

MATERIALS/SUGGESTED YARN

Many patterns will be designed to work specifically with a named yarn. Many yarn companies have in-house designers who work with that company's yarns to produce patterns (for free or for sale in books and magazines) that consumers will want to knit and so drive up their yarn sales. Independent designers will often specify the yarn that they worked with when developing a pattern, as they can then be certain that that yarn 'works' with that pattern.

Using a different yarn from the one suggested

There may be times when a knitter is either not able to purchase the particular yarn specified in a pattern, or wishes to substitute it for other reasons — such as the wish to use a vegan-approved yarn, or for greater ease of care of the finished item. In these circumstances it becomes necessary to substitute the named yarn for another one.

There are two important points to take note of when choosing a substitute yarn:

Gauge

Check that the gauge on the ball band of the substitute yarn is equal to that of the named yarn (see ball band diagram on page 19). The gauge given on a ball band most often shows the number of stitches per 10cm needed to make a medium density, medium drape fabric. By matching this drape and density with the original yarn there is a greater chance of matching the fabric characteristics of the author's original garment.

Yarn properties

If the designer has chosen a smooth and inelastic yarn such as silk for their pattern, then substituting this yarn with a springy rustic tweed yarn will result in a finished project with very different physical properties from the original intentions of the designer. Consulting the guide to different yarn types (see pages 7–15) when choosing a substitute yarn with different fibre content will help to select an alternative yarn with similar physical properties.

NEEDLE SIZE

Patterns will almost always specify which needles the designer suggests will get a knitter close to matching a pattern's gauge (page 4). However, it is always extremely important to remember that the needle size is just a suggestion, and will not be the correct needle size to suit all knitters. The needle size given is only that which the designer used to achieve the specified gauge, so the knitter following the pattern may achieve a completely different gauge using this size needle and may need to use a needle one or more sizes larger or smaller to achieve correct gauge.

TOOLS AND NOTIONS

If any tools other than knitting needles are needed to complete the pattern, they should also be listed. Many patterns will not list the most common knitting tools (such as a ruler for measuring gauge, scissors for cutting yarn and a tapestry needle for weaving in ends) but if an item such as a crochet hook or stitch markers are needed, then these will usually be listed towards the beginning of the pattern.

Pocket Tip

A small and handy alternative to carrying a pair of scissors in a travelling knitting kit is to keep a small seam ripper in the knitting bag. A 'seam ripper' is a small tool used to undo stitched seams on sewn garments, often shaped like a small ballpoint pen and about 10cm long. It contains a little pointed end and a small curved cutting surface: perfect for cutting yarn ends. Seam rippers are very inexpensive and can be found in any haberdashery.

SIZING

Patterns for items of clothing will very often include several sizing options. Measure the intended recipient for the best fit – do not be tempted to guess! Some patterns may also give information on the amount of ease the finished garment is to have.

Pocket Fact ☺

A jumper knitted to fit a 336 inch chest was machine knitted by factory workers in China to beat the record for the world's largest sweater.

Ease descriptions:

- **No ease.** A sweater knitted with no ease will be close-fitting without being tight. It will follow the lines of the body but will not be restrictive.

- **Positive ease.** The amount of positive ease noted in a pattern denotes how much extra 'room' there will be in the finished article. If a sweater pattern specifies that it should have 10cm of positive ease then the circumference of the jumper will be 10cm larger than that of the person wearing it. A jumper with a lot of positive ease will be relaxed and 'baggy'.

- **Negative ease.** Many knitted fabrics, especially those knitted from wool and other fibres with a bit of 'give' (see pages 15–16 for fibre types and properties) have the ability to stretch. It is this property of knitted fabric that allows garments to be knitted with negative ease. A garment knitted with negative ease is intended to fit tightly against the body and closely follow the lines of the figure. The amount of negative ease given by a pattern denotes how much smaller the finished item is intended to be in comparison to the person wearing it. If a pattern says the finished item is to have 6cm of negative ease, then that item will have to stretch 6cm to fit the person wearing it, so that the knitted fabric sits closely against the skin.

Pattern sizes

If a pattern includes instructions for multiple sizes it will usually list all but the smallest size in parenthesis. For example, if a hat is available in three sizes; child, teen and

adult, these will usually be written as 'child (teen, adult)'.
When the pattern carries any instructions where the number of
stitches worked differs according to the size being knitted, the
same pattern will be followed, such as in the instruction 'knit
10 (12, 14)'. In this example, anyone following the
instructions for knitting a teen-sized hat should follow the
numbers given as the first number within the parenthesis.

ABBREVIATIONS

Knitting patterns will often carry a list of knitting stitch abbreviations. Often, patterns will only specifically list non-standard or unusual knitting stitches, or give definitions of special knitting techniques – such as how to knit a particular cable stitch.

Knitting patterns usually employ a standard set of knitting abbreviations and terms which may seem complex at first, but a knitter will usually find they learn almost by accident within time. Though it may seem frustrating to have to keep referring to a knitting abbreviations key at first, reading and recognising these terms becomes second nature after a while and so the proportion of time spent between understanding a pattern and actually knitting soon swings heavily in favour of the more enjoyable task.

A list of standard terms and abbreviations can be found on pages 97–99.

Pocket Fact ☺

An incredible 150,000 knitting patterns had been logged and
categorised in popular knitting website Ravelry's database,
www.ravelry.com, at the start of 2011.

PATTERN INSTRUCTIONS

The most important part of a knitting pattern is the set of instructions for actually knitting the garment. This set of instructions may be presented in a number of different ways, so it is extremely important to always read through the pattern to the very end, (like an exam paper) before committing your stitches to your needles. Unlike an exam, nobody will grade your knitting progress and the clock is not ticking down with every passing second, so it's always worth a knitter taking their time to fully understand the instructions before casting on.

Knitting pattern instructions are usually written in chronological order, a line or section at a time. However, sometimes a pattern designer will leave out what they deem to be unnecessary instructions. For example, many lace patterns will simply instruct the knitter to purl every even-numbered (or wrong side) row, rather than write the same instruction for every second row of the pattern. This leaves the pattern uncluttered and saves both space and paper. Another space saving device employed by pattern writers is the use of abbreviations, as noted in the accompanying list of abbreviations (see pages 97–99).

Repeat instructions

Often, a pattern will use a form of shorthand when describing sets of stitches that are repeated. These are usually shown within parenthesis or between asterisks.

If a line of a pattern carries the instruction: p4, (k10, p5) 3 times, k4, it is giving the instruction that the knitter should knit four stitches, repeat the instructions in the brackets three times, and then knit four more stitches. Written without the short hand in parenthesis the same instruction would read: p4, k10, p5, k10, p5, k10, p5, k4.

CHARTS

Some patterns, especially those for knitted lace or those that use a lot of cable stitches, will be presented in the form of a chart. There are a few tips to remember when reading knitting charts:

- Charts are always read from the bottom line up. This is because the first row of stitches that are knitted will be at the bottom of the knitted piece. When knitting a scarf, for example, the knitting 'grows' from the top, as new rows of knitting are added to the upper part of the knitted rectangle.

- The first line of a chart is usually read from right to left. This is the standard way of presenting a chart as when knitting a row of stitches it is the rightmost stitches that are worked on first.

- After this, things get slightly more complicated. If the item being knitted is constructed to be knitted in the round (pages 66–69) – such as when knitting a hat or socks, or anything else with a cylindrical, tubular construction – then all lines of the chart will usually be knitted from right to left, as the piece of knitting will always be going in the same direction. However, if the pattern is for an item that is to be knitted flat (knit back and forth in rows, such as a scarf might be) then even-numbered rows will often be presented from left to right, so that the charts shows the work from the correct (or 'public') side.

SCHEMATIC

Patterns for knitted items with a number of separate pieces that need to be joined together after knitting, or which feature an unusual construction, will sometimes include a schematic. This handy diagram is designed to help a knitter visualise what part of a pattern they are knitting and how all of the pieces will fit together after knitting. It is also useful for ensuring that all of the knitted pieces are coming out the right shape, so that there are no nasty surprises when it comes to sewing the garment up and a knitter suddenly discovers that their cardigan has two necklines and only one sleeve.

BLOCKING DIAGRAM/BLOCKING INFORMATION

Similar to the schematic, a blocking diagram is a pictorial representation of the knitted item. The purpose of the blocking diagram, however, is to give the proposed final dimensions of the knitted piece. As knitting has the ability to increase in size when being blocked, the blocking diagram shows the finished dimensions that the pieces of knitting should be pinned to whilst they dry or are steam-treated.

Pocket Fact ☺

An item such as a lace shawl can grow to more than twice its original dimensions when blocked. Blocking lace can result in a fantastic effort-to-wow ratio.

COPYRIGHT AND COMPANY INFORMATION

The pattern will usually include a copyright notice and details of the company or individual that has produced the pattern.

Pattern errors

As with any printed publication, mistakes occasionally creep into a published pattern. When this happens the publishers will usually publish a list of errata. Knitters should always check for any errata before casting on for a project. With periodical publications such as magazines, these errata are usually found in the following issue, or online if the publication has an accompanying website. Mistakes in patterns from books and from the internet are usually found online.

Another way to discover if a pattern has any errors in it is to search for that pattern online. Many members of the large online knitting communities like to document their progress on social knitting sites and blogs. If a certain pattern returns lots of search results with people complaining that the finished knitted piece is lacking a hole for the head, it can be assumed that there is a mistake somewhere in the pattern that the braver knitter may attempt to work around, and the more cautious may decide to contact the pattern author about.

KNITTING PATTERN ABBREVIATIONS

beg	begin, beginning
b/o	bind off
c/o	cast on
circ	circular/circular needle
cn	cable needle
cont	continue
dec	decrease
DPN/DPNs	double pointed needle(s)
inc	increase
K	knit
K2tog	knit two together: a decrease stitch Knit two stitches together as if they were one single stitch by inserting your right needle into the front leg of both stitches and knitting them together. This turns two stitches into a single stitch, so decreasing by one stitch.
K3tog	knit three together: a decrease stitch Knit three stitches together as if they were one single stitch by inserting your right needle into the front leg of all three stitches and knitting them together. This turns three stitches into a single stitch, so decreasing by two stitches.
Kfb	knit front and back: an increase stitch Knit into the front of a stitch and without dropping the stitch from the left needle, knit into the back leg of it. This increases by one stitch.
kwise	Knit-wise: as if to knit This is often said when slipping a stitch from the left needle to the right without working it. Insert the right needle into the next stitch as if you are about to knit it, and then simply slip it on to the right needle.

m	marker (stitch marker)
MI	make one stitch This is an instruction telling you to increase by one stitch. This direction doesn't give instructions on how to perform the increase, but the most common increased used with this instruction is MIL (see below).
MIL	make one left: a left-slanting increase Insert left needle under the strand or 'bar' between needles from the front. Knit into the back of this lifted bar, so creating a new stitch.
MIR	make one right: a right-slanting increase Insert left needle under the strand or 'bar' between needles from the back. Knit into the front of this lifted bar, so creating a new stitch.
P	purl
pm	place marker Place stitch marker to track the beginning of a round or section of the knitting pattern.
psso	pass slipped stitch over Use the tip of the left needle to pass the slipped stitch over subsequent knit stitches and off the needle.
pwise	purl-wise: as if to purl This is often said when slipping a stitch from the left needle to the right without working it. Insert the right needle into the next stitch as if you are about to purl it, and then simply slip it on to the right needle.
rnd	round
rs	right side

SKP/SKPO	slip, knit, pass: a decrease stitch Slip one stitch, knit the next stitch, and then pass the slipped stitch over the knitted stitch and off the needle.
sl	slip
sm	slip marker Slip stitch marker from the left to right needle.
SSK	slip, slip, knit: a decrease stitch Slip one stitch knit-wise, then another stitch, and then knit them together using the left needle.
st/sts	stitch/stitches
stst	stockinette stitch
tbl	through back loop (through the back 'leg' of the stitch)
tog	together
ws	wrong side
wyib	with yarn in back An instruction to keep working yarn at the back of the work: often used as an instruction when slipping stitches from one needle to another.
wyif	with yarn in front An instruction to keep working yarn at the back of the work: often used as an instruction when slipping stitches from one needle to another.
YF	yarn forward Bring yarn forward between the two needles.
YO	yarn over Bring yarn forward between the two needles, ready to knit next stitch.

🕷 FINDING A PROJECT 🕷

It is often said that there are two types of knitters: process knitters and project knitters. Process knitters knit purely for the joy of knitting and for the journey that knitting takes them on, from ball of yarn to finished object. The joy of creating and the occupation of the hands being enough of a reason for such knitters to churn out stitch after stitch of knitted fabric, working their way through metre after metre of yarn.

Project knitters, on the other hand, knit for the joy of the finished object – whether to own and wear that object, or draw admiration for their talent from other people or their own satisfaction.

Whether these two hypothesised 'types' of knitter are so clearly delineated is unsure, as for many people an item knitted with joy is likely to become a treasured knitted piece much of the time. Whether a knitter brings their needles and yarn together for the pleasure of knitting or because they wish to own a cardigan or beret with very specific design features, part of the journey from the desire to knit to a finished object must include the search for the perfect pattern.

WHERE TO FIND PATTERNS

The popularity of knitting in the last century was somewhat hindered by the availability of patterns. Before the advent of the instant information delivery made possible by the internet, knitting patterns had to be bought in paper form and in booklets, magazines or single-sheet patterns, mostly from specialist vendors. As there was a limit to the number of patterns that a shop could stock and sell, it made sense to stock those designs thought to be most mainstream and commercial – meaning knitters were restricted to a certain number of patterns. Now that knitting has seen a sharp upsurge in popularity though, there is a whole plethora of ways to discover new and interesting patterns to knit and enjoy.

Books

Knitting books often present a thrifty way to purchase patterns: the price of a book being equivalent to far fewer individually purchased patterns. Some books will offer a range of different projects from various designers, but many will be focused around a particular theme – either a style of knitwear (such as romantic or rustic knits), based around a particular skill or knitting tradition (such as Estonian lace or stranded colourwork), or around a particular type of knitted item (such as books about knitting socks or hats).

Pocket Fact ☺

Online shopping store Amazon lists almost 17,000 book titles under the category of knitting.

Magazines

An alternative source of printed patterns is to be found in the increasing number of knitting magazines available on the news-stands. Knitting magazines often feature a smaller but more diverse selection of patterns than might be found in knitting books. One benefit of knitting magazines is that if a subscription is taken out (thus usually making the magazine itself cheaper to buy) a surprise selection of patterns will arrive through the letterbox every month. This may also be a downside, however, if the knitter is not keen on that month's selection of tissue-box cosies and cat jumpers.

Here a look at some of the following:

● *The Knitter*

● *Simply Knitting*

● *Yarn Forward*

● *Vogue Knitting*

● *Debbie Bliss*

Pattern booklets, leaflets and single-issue patterns

Many yarn shops and department stores will carry a selection of patterns issued by yarn companies to accompany their yarn collections. Sometimes these are single patterns, or issued in collections, and arranged either by style or designer.

For example:

- Rowan magazine and collections
- Louisa Harding
- Kaffe Fassett

The information superhighway

Now that the internet has become a worldwide information storage and trade solution, there are hardly any boundaries to what a knitter might find a pattern for. From vintage and classic sweaters to items that would make a sailor blush, there really is something for every knitter.

Some good places to search for patterns to download online include:

- Knitting blogs and personal websites
- Knitting and crochet community sites such as Ravelry, www.ravelry.com
- Online craft marketplaces such as Etsy, www.etsy.com, and Folksy, www.folksy.com

Online yarn stores may offer paper patterns to purchase and be delivered by post, but electronically delivered patterns are becoming increasingly popular for both their convenience and speed of delivery (many downloads will be instantaneous), with the added benefit that electronic files do not require postage to be paid. There are many thousands of patterns available for either a small electronic payment (via credit or debit card payment, or other online payment solution) or even for free from some companies and independent designers.

Pocket Fact ☺

The largest online fibre-lovers community site, www.ravelry.com, has over 150,000 knitting patterns listed in its database. Of these, over 100,000 are available for instant download and immediate knitting gratification.

Second-hand/charity shops

Many charity shops carry a selection of used and vintage patterns. Though the kindest thing that can be said for many of these patterns is that they are quaintly retro, they are usually very inexpensive and are an interesting piece of social history. Charity store pattern collections also sometimes contain a hidden gem in their dusty boxes – a pattern for a classic design or stunning piece of lace, for example.

Pocket Tip ✄

It is important to be wary of a few things when knitting from vintage patterns. Firstly, take care to make note of the needle size – many will often use the (now mostly outdated) British needle size system (see page 4), so it may be necessary to consult a needle size conversion chart (one of these can be found on page 5)

Additionally, the size and proportions of the average human body have changed drastically in the last few decades, so be sure to check the measurements carefully before casting on.

🪡 WHAT TO KNIT 🪡

Often, one of the most enjoyable aspects of knitting is looking through all of the available patterns in the hunt for what to knit. As with embarking upon any new project, there are a few considerations to take into account when selecting a pattern.

DIFFICULTY LEVEL

Some patterns will list a difficulty level to help guide prospective knitters into the amount of knitting knowledge they may need to complete the project. Though many knitters may only feel comfortable in choosing a pattern that uses techniques from within their skill set, it is important to remember that progression only comes from stepping outside the comfort zone in order to learn new things. If a knitter does want to learn a new technique, such as colourwork or cabling, it may be advisable to pick a small accessory project to practise the new technique with.

Difficulty grading

The Craft Yarn Council (www.craftyarncouncil.com) has sought to devise industry-wide standards when grading knitting pattern difficulty, dividing projects into four difficulty levels: Beginner, Easy, Intermediate and Advanced.

Under this system:
- *Beginner projects are classed as those that are mostly composed of simple knit and purl stitches with minimal shaping.*
- *Easy projects are defined as those using basic stitches and shaping, simple colour changes (such as stripes) and repetitive, easy to remember stitch patterns.*
- *Intermediate patterns may incorporate cables and lace, simple colourwork (intarsia and stranded, see Glossary pages 162 and 166) knitting in-the-round and a reasonable amount of shaping.*
- *Advanced level patterns are those judged to be suited to more experienced knitters, and may include use of intricate lace or cable work, complex colourwork or shaping in the form of short rows.*

Though this is a handy 'rough guide' to pattern difficulty levels, it is important to note that despite the Craft Yarn Council's best intentions, there is no accepted standard when classifying pattern difficulty level, and many companies and designers will simply devise their own system of difficulty — and much of the time will not provide a key to their classification system. Knitters can always read through the instructions to assess whether the pattern is within their skill set.

YARN AVAILABILITY AND STASH

Some knitters will go through life without accruing a stash, whereas others will not be able to turn down a bargain or beautiful skein of yarn when spotted upon a yarn store shelf. The former kind of knitter possibly has it easier when trying to match yarn to project. They will first find a pattern that they wish to knit and then go on the hunt for the appropriate yarn. The only problem with this is that the stash-less knitter is less likely to be able to find a bargain when searching for a particular yarn, unless they happen to strike it lucky.

A knitter with a stash has a slightly different problem. Though they may be blessed with a yarn mountain that they have to climb over every morning just to get out of bed, they will sometimes feel guilt-ridden into trying to knit projects only using the yarn that they have already purchased. This can sometimes lead to less than perfect yarn-to-project match-ups and unhappy knitters with itchy sweaters. A temporary solution may be to buy more yarn for this project and so not chip away at Mt. Wool.

Pocket Fact ☺

Twine features in a number of knitting patterns, especially those for floor mats and market bags. The world's largest ball of twine can be found in Cawker City, Kansas, USA. Started in 1953 and still being added to today by townsfolk and tourists alike, the twine currently measures over $2\frac{1}{2}$ million metres long and weighs close to 5,000kg.

⚹ KNITTING FOR OTHERS ⚹

Once the knitting bug bites it is natural to want to share the fruits of the time spent knitting with friends and loved ones, both because a knitter understands the quality and value of a hand-knitted item and because they wish to show their loved ones how much they are cherished by spending the extra time and effort on making something specifically for them.

Inevitably, though, not all people are equally understanding of the value of a hand-knitted piece. The charm of a hand-knit may be lost on some people who are fully immersed in modern consumer culture, preferring big brand names to lovingly created hand-knits, and leaves the knitter wishing that they'd not wasted their time. Sometimes knitting for others may seem like a bit of a mine-field, but there are ways of lessening the danger of an unloved hand-knit, or, at least, cushioning the blow.

START SMALL

It is perhaps not a good idea for a knitter to jump straight in at the deep end and start knitting jumpers that require large amounts of time and skill to give as first knitted gifts. Some people don't like huge knitted jumpers, some people don't like chartreuse eyelash yarn, and (as crazy as it may sound) some people just don't like hand-knits, no matter how well-crafted and on trend they may be.

There is no single rule as to who will cherish their hand knit for-ever and who will line their cat-basket with it, so a little recon-naissance work may be in order. If the gift recipient is to be seen swathed in hand-knit clothes on a regular basis, then they are like-ly to respond well to the generous gift of a knitted item. If the recipient does not usually revel in a world of hand knits, however, it may be a good idea to start with smaller gifts and see how well they are received before tackling more ambitious gift projects.

DON'T GIVE AN ALBATROSS

When deciding upon a project to give to someone who doesn't knit, it is important to take into consideration the care requirements of the object. Beautifully knitted items of fine merino wool have a chance of being ruined beyond repair by busy people who are likely to throw the item in the washing machine with the rest of their weekly load. This isn't meant out of disrespect to the knitter. People are so used to the easy care requirements of shop-bought garments that it is all too easy to forget that a hand knit often requires extra care and handling. Look for man-made fibres or Superwash wool when giving hand-knits, so that the finished items may be easily cared for and durable.

DON'T GIVE A LIABILITY

Closely linked with the sentiments above, if a knitted gift made of luxury, high-maintenance fibres is given, there is a danger that the recipient will come to view the gift as something of a liability. Warnings and instructions on how to best care for the item may be given when handing over the gift, but there is a danger that this will scare the recipient off from ever wearing or washing the item, for fear of ruining the knitter's handiwork.

DON'T GIVE YOUR HEART ALONG WITH YOUR KNITTING

Perhaps the most important consideration is not to be too precious about knitted gifts. It is almost vital to realise early on that not all knitted gifts are going to be a hit. Some will be buried away in the back of a drawer or mysteriously 'lost'. This can be frustrating and even upsetting at times, and the best way for a knitter to guard against this is to not spend too much time, money and effort on giving a knitted gift until they can be sure that the recipient is appreciative of hand-knitted items.

🧶 A PROJECT FOR (MOST) PEOPLE 🧶

Matching a project to a recipient can be tricky, and sometimes a knitter should concede that there may not be a perfect pattern out there for everyone, but here are a few starting ideas that may just spark the imagination.

PARTNER

A knitter's partner, if they have one, is probably the person best known to them, and so is perhaps the easiest and yet most difficult person to knit for. It is natural for a knitter to want to make the most elaborate items for the person that they care for most, but it is always wise to take a step back and consider if that person likes elaborate knitwear, or plainer, more understated knits. Small love tokens in the way of desk mascots and small, humorous knitted creatures often strike a good note as a memento between two partners.

FATHER/OLDER MALE FAMILY MEMBERS

Always the hardest people to buy gifts for, let alone knit for, dads have a habit of muttering something about needing more socks every time their birthday approaches. As it happens, socks are one of the most popular types of item to knit and there are many thousands of sock patterns available. It may be advisable to skip the bright fuchsia lace footsies and aim for something more rugged and hardwearing – a stockinette stitch sock will please most people, with a cable or two thrown in for embellishment if the recipient likes a little bit of extra detail in their clothing.

Pocket Tip

Knitted socks can have less 'give' in them than thin, shop-bought cotton socks. If the intended recipient of a pair of socks has mobility problems that may affect the ease with which they put on their socks, use a yarn with some elastane content. Elastane will help with the ease of putting on the socks and stop them from falling down around the ankle.

Other ideas for older male recipients include:

- Hats

- Gloves

- Felted slippers

- Mug cosies

- Hot water bottle covers

- Sofa-arm remote control organiser pocket

MOTHER/OLDER FEMALE FAMILY MEMBERS

Every stylish woman deserves a scarf to wrap around their neck and highlight their face, and a unique, hand-knitted scarf can set just about any outfit off beautifully. From warm, winter scarves to delicate lace scarves perfect for garden parties and spring weddings, a scarf is the ultimate accessory. A step on from this is the shawl. Often triangular in shape, but sometimes circular or semi-circular, or shaped like a rectangular stole, a shawl can be worn around the neck, draped across the shoulders, tied about the torso or even worn around the waist and hips with a summer dress.

Pocket Fact ☺

A team of charity knitters in Wales broke a world record in 2005 by knitting a scarf over 53km (33 miles) long.

Other ideas for female recipients include:

- Gloves
- Homeware items such as cushion covers
- Socks
- Bags
- Cowl
- Luxury facecloths (nice when given with a bar of handmade soap)

YOUNGER MALE FAMILY MEMBERS

Young males can be difficult to knit for, especially around the teenage years when trying to work out what is and isn't fashionable in their eyes is all but impossible. Younger boys may be charmed with knitted toys and puzzles (there are a number of knitted Rubik's style puzzles available) and older males often take kindly to simple knitted beanie-style hats.

A few ideas to consider for younger males include:

- Gadget cosies for MP3 players and portable gaming consoles
- Simple hats in understated colours

- Scientific-style knitted models
- Simple length-wise striped scarves
- Fingerless gloves
- Novelty items such as knitted beards and Viking helmets

YOUNGER FEMALE FAMILY MEMBERS

Knitting for younger females is usually slightly easier then knitting for males as long as it is always remembered that a teenage girl's fashion ideas change at lightning speed. For this reason it is recommended that a knitter does not spend more than a few weeks on any given project as the girl in question is likely to have changed her mind on whether it is fashionable by the time it is sewn together and presented to her, her sullen face proclaiming that it is so, like, last month.

Younger girls often appreciate gifts of small knitted purses and handbags to keep their valuables in, as well as toys and hair accessories.

A few ideas to consider for younger females:

- Fingerless mittens/hand-warmers
- Hair accessories
- Gadget holder
- Hats
- Bags
- Soft toys

Pocket Fact ☺

Amigurumi is the Japanese art of knitting or crocheting small, anthropomorphic animal figures. The emphasis of many amigurumi patterns is on cute, rounded shapes with over-sized heads and wide-eyed expressions.

WORK COLLEAGUES AND OTHER ACQUAINTANCES

Sometimes it may happen that a knitter feels the need to spread their knitted goodness in a circle wider than the usual set of friends and family, perhaps due to a gift exchange (most often for 'Secret Santa'), or because a colleague is leaving work for pastures new. Gift knitting can be difficult when it is for casual or non-personal acquaintances, but items that can be quickly knitted and used around the office environment may go down well.

If the recipient is always crowding around the coffee machine, mug in hand, a mug cosy will be a welcome gift (see the pattern on page 131). If the colleague prefers to bring their coffee in from a local coffee shop, a paper cup cosy will help the insulation of their drink from the shop to the office and also help save the environment: guarding against the need to use a corrugated cardboard cup sleeve every day.

OTHER PEOPLE'S BABIES

If an expectant parent knows a knitter they will ask that knitter to make something for their impending arrival. Often the prospective parent, swelling both in joy and tummy, will not for one second dream of the possibility that the knitter may not want to spend hours of every evening knitting a full layette set and a menagerie of knitted toys for their baby. If a knitter wants to get off the baby-knitting train, it is imperative that they do so as soon as the subject is breached, otherwise they should cancel their holidays and book time off work. If, however, the knitter wishes to take on some baby knitting, there is a wealth of ideas to make for impending little bundles.

Here are but a few projects:

- Baby blankets
- Cardigans
- Bootees

- Baby socks
- Soft toys
- Baby hats

Points to consider when knitting for babies

There are a number of careful considerations to make when knitting for babies, most of which concern safety. Buttons can come loose unless well attached, fringing and pompoms may shed short lengths of yarn, and any drawstring poses a risk should the baby become entangled.

Soft toys should be well assembled and have any limbs etc securely sewn on, or (ideally) be knitted in one piece. Safety eyes/noses are not recommended for young children, so toy features should be embroidered on.

Baby items are likely to need regular laundering, so easy-care yarns can be helpful, though some people disagree with the use of acrylic for baby clothing. You could also look at using especially soft or non-irritant yarns such as cashmerino, but it is best to find out the parents' wishes on what fibres they will be dressing their baby in before embarking on any knitting.

I-CORD

Elizabeth Zimmerman's i-cord makes for a fantastic embellishment as it can be used for decorative appliqué work or to create ties and rope-like cords to finish hats and many other knitted projects. I-cords are often included in hat patterns for babies but knitters must take care that there is no danger posed by the cord or any other kind of tie (see box above).

The i-cord (short for idiot cord, as Zimmerman could hardly believe that she has 'unvented' it, as she put it) is identical in structure to the knitted cords formed by using a knitting dolly or wooden cotton reel with four nails hammered in one end, but is instead formed with two DPN needles.

To knit an i-cord

1. Cast on three or four stitches (depending on the desired thickness of the i-cord), onto one of the DPN needles.

2. Using the other DPN, knit all stitches.

3. Do *not* turn work. Instead place the needle with the stitches into the left hand with the working yarn emerging from the left-most stitch.

4 Using the empty DPN, knit all stitches, pulling working yarn taught after the first stitch.

Repeat steps 3 and 4 until the i-cord measures the desired length, then bind off all stitches.

I-cord can be knitted from more than four stitches, but when the stitch count amounts to five stitches or more a 'ladder' often forms due to the working yarn having to stretch across the back of so many stitches to reach the first stitch. As with most knitting techniques and ideas, it doesn't hurt to give it a go and the knitting can always be unravelled if the effect isn't appreciated.

🪡 CARING FOR HAND KNITS 🪡

Hand-knitted items can require a little more care and gentler handling than mass-manufactured garments, but this is highly dependent on the fibre content and intended use of the individual item.

Acrylic items can be machine-washed and usually tumble-dried without any fears of this adversely affecting the finished item (in fact, many knitters believe that tumble-drying acrylic items softens them considerably).

Items made from natural fibres may require considerably more care. Large hand-knitted items such as sweaters and other garments should usually be dried flat, to prevent stretching due to the weight of evaporating water. Mesh screens that fit over the bathtub are manufactured for just such a purpose.

Lace and other items that require blocking when knitted will require the same treatment every time they are laundered. Thankfully, lace items do not usually require regular washing.

The ball band on a ball of the yarn used should give care instructions on how to best care for garments made out of that yarn.

Pocket Tip ✂

Knitters should not be tempted to rely on memory alone when laundering hand-knitted garments. Keeping the ball band from any yarns used will help keep track of how to care for a hand-knit wardrobe. Alternatively, details of garment care might be kept in a small notebook or file, along with spare lengths of yarn and extra buttons, should any repairs need to be made in the future.

GIFT KNITS AND FUTURE CARE

When a knitter gives a hand knit made from a high-maintenance fibre as a gift, they run the risk of that item being spoiled if they do not impart adequate care advice along with the present. One way to avoid this is to make an accompanying gift tag with full care instructions. Punching a hole in the top of this gift tag will allow it to be slipped over the hook of a coat hanger, so that the laundering instructions may always be kept with any larger garments.

Pocket Tip ✂

If a gift knit features buttons, it is a good idea to purchase one or more spare buttons at the time of knitting, in case one gets lost. Any spare buttons may be sewn to an accompanying care instruction gift card so that all care items are kept together.

AVOIDING PESTS

One of the direst fates that might befall a knitted garment is that it falls foul of wool-loving pests. Moths are the best known of the wool-munchers, but there are a number of other household pests such as carpet beetles and their larval form, 'woolly bears'.

Though it is impossible to fully guard against succumbing to such pests, there are a few ways to at least help lessen the chance of a wool-loving invasion.

Mothballs

Mothballs are a traditional form of moth repellent and work as a result of the chemicals naphthalene and paradichlorobenzene. Mothballs give off vapours that, in sufficient concentration, will slowly kill wool- and silk-loving pests. The vapours only build up to the required concentration in an airtight environment though. This makes them handy for long-term storage where knitwear is not used for two or three seasons, but less effective in wardrobes and drawer systems, which are not airtight and are regularly opened. When used in non-airtight environments the concentration only weakly repels adult larvae, and any established larvae will continue to feed.

Mothballs are also poisonous to both humans and animals, so must be kept away from children and pets, and leave a distinctive (many would say unpleasant) smell which lingers on clothes and is difficult to remove, even with washing.

Prevention

Moths are repelled by light, and only stay loosely nestled in between layers of clothing. A good preventive tactic to stop moths moving in is to periodically remove items from wardrobes and chests of drawers and give them a good and thorough shake. Some people use cedar balls and cedar chests believing that the oil in cedar wood helps with pests. Cedar wood is a repellent to insects, but only a mild one, and shouldn't be used as a sole preventive measure.

To best guard against insects that may ruin cherished knitwear, keep items sealed in airtight containers and vacuum-sealed bags where possible, and inspect all knitwear regularly for signs of holes or droppings.

What to do if moths get in

If a knitter does discover that they have fallen foul to voracious moth appetites, it is natural to start to feel a sense of rising panic. A calm and methodical approach may do more to save the knitwear, though. If holes are found in knitted items, try not to disturb the site of the broken fibres too much – the knitwear may be able to be rescued (see Chapter 7 for more on fixing mistakes).

Pocket Fact ☺

Killerton House stately home in Devon was subjected to a ferocious attack of clothes moths that began breeding three times a year instead of the usual one, due to warm temperatures in 2007. The moths had a taste for fine (and very old) fibres, and munched their way through many priceless and irreplaceable furnishings and clothing artefacts.

All items should then be washed in hot water of 65°C or an even higher temperature. Naturally, some knitwear will not like this and will shrink into a firm doormat of doll-sized proportions. When dealing with items that are likely to be ruined by hot water, an alternative tactic is to put the garments in separate airtight freezer bags and put them in the deep freeze for two to three days before defrosting and washing in a gentler manner. Both these extremes of temperature should kill moths in all stages of the life cycle (egg, larvae, pupae and adult).

It is important to rid the rest of the house of infestation, too. Carpets and upholstery are particularly susceptible – these should be vacuumed and cleaned. Wardrobes and drawers should also be thoroughly vacuumed and washed before knitwear is put back.

Pocket Fact ☺

The world's first knitting machine was invented in 1589 by an English clergyman, William Lee. Modern knitting machines use the same basic mechanical principles as Lee's original design but Queen Elizabeth I originally refused to allow a patent for William Lee's original invention of the knitting machine on the grounds that it would put hand-knitters out of business.

5

PATTERNS

Each of the patterns included in this book introduce techniques for a different style of knitting. The skills needed to complete each pattern are listed at the beginning of each design. None of the patterns included are very difficult, and each should be an enjoyable knit. If you are confused about any of the techniques used in these patterns, simply consult the Glossary and the relevant sections of the book for help. Measurements for each of the patterns are given in centimetres; if you'd rather work in inches, please use our handy centimetre-to-inch conversion chart on page 169. For tips on where to find the yarns used in these patterns see pages 21–22.

Have a look at the colour section in the centre of the book for pictures of the finished patterns.

✄ HOLLY'S HANDWARMERS ✄

These charming fingerless gloves are the perfect accessory. They keep the palm of the hand toasty warm whilst leaving the fingers free to search around for bus fare or send that all-important text message. They are also the perfect gift for the would-be author as they keep the hands warm whilst the fingers are free to rush around the keyboard at high speed.

These handwarmers feature a very simple construction and are knitted as a flat rectangle, which is them sewn into a glove with a thumb opening. The gloves require no shaping and are composed solely of knit and purl stitches, and so are a perfect beginner's project or a very fast knit for a more experienced knitter.

The gloves are made in super-stretchy 1×1 ribbing, which will hug and warm the hand and ensure a good fit, whilst also featuring smooth stockinette panels with moss stitch diamonds for decoration and interest.

MATERIALS

Rowan Pure Wool DK, 2 × 50g balls

NEEDLES

3.75mm (US size 5) straight needles

NOTIONS

Large, blunt-ended tapestry needle for sewing up

GAUGE

- Stitch gauge: 23 stitches per 10cm in stretched 1×1 ribbing

- Row gauge: 30 stitches per 10cm in 1×1 ribbing

FINISHED MEASUREMENTS

Made to fit a 15cm–20cm hand circumference. The 1×1 ribbing used in this pattern means that the mittens are wonderfully stretchy.

ABBREVIATIONS

- c/o = cast on
- k = knit
- p = purl
- b/o = bind off

SKILLS NEEDED TO COMPLETE THIS PATTERN

- Casting on
- Knit and purl stitches
- Yarn overs
- Binding off

INSTRUCTIONS (MAKE TWO OF THESE)

Leaving a 50cm tail of yarn for seaming, loosely c/o 42 stitches.

Rows 1–20: (k1, p1) to end.

Row 21: (k1, p1) 3 times, k11, (p1, k1) 4 times, p1, k11, (p1, k1) twice, p1.

Row 22: (k1, p1) twice, k1, p11, (k1, p1) 4 times, k1, p11, (k1, p1) 3 times.

Row 23: (k1, p1) 3 times, k5, p1, k5, (p1, k1) 4 times, (p1, k5) twice, (p1, k1) twice, p1.

Row 24: (k1, p1) twice, k1, p4, k1, p1, k1, p4, (k1, p1) 4 times, k1, p4, k1, p1, k1, p4, (k1, p1) 3 times.

Row 25: (k1, p1) 3 times, k3, (p1, k1) twice, p1, k3, (p1, k1) 4 times, p1, k3, (p1, k1) twice, p1, k3, (p1, k1) twice, p1.

Row 26: (k1, p1) twice, k1, p2 (k1, p1) 3 times, k1, p2, (k1, p1) 4 times, k1, p2 (k1, p1) 3 times, k1, p2, (k1, p1) 3 times.

Row 27: (k1, p1) to end.

Row 28: (k1, p1) twice, k1, p2 (k1, p1) 3 times, k1, p2, (k1, p1) 4 times, k1, p2 (k1, p1) 3 times, k1, p2, (k1, p1) 3 times.

Row 29: (k1, p1) to end.

Row 30: (k1, p1) twice, k1, p2 (k1, p1) 3 times, k1, p2, (k1, p1) 4 times, k1, p2 (k1, p1) 3 times, k1, p2, (k1, p1) 3 times.

Row 31: (k1, p1) 3 times, k3, (p1, k1) twice, p1, k3, (p1, k1) 4 times, p1, k3, (p1, k1) twice, p1, k3, (p1, k1) twice, p1.

Row 32: (k1, p1) twice, k1, p4, k1, p1, k1, p4, (k1, p1) 4 times, k1, p4, k1, p1, k1, p4, (k1, p1) 3 times.

Row 33: (k1, p1) 3 times, k5, p1, k5, (p1, k1) 4 times, (p1, k5) twice, (p1, k1) twice, p1.

Row 34: (k1, p1) twice, k1, p11, (k1, p1) 4 times, k1, p11, (k1, p1) 3 times.

Rows 35–48: Repeat rows 21–34.

Row 49: (k1, p1) 3 times, k11, (p1, k1) 4 times, p1, k11, (p1, k1) twice, p1.

Rows 50–59: (k1, p1) to end.

Cut yarn, leaving a 50cm tail for sewing up. Do not weave in ends.

Block both mittens to a width of 15cm to preserve stretchiness of ribbing.

Using a blunt-ended knitters' sewing-up needle and the tail of yarn left when casting on, fold each glove in half, side to side, and sew up the ribbed portion of the bottom cuff, stopping when the bottom of the decorative panel is reached. Cut yarn leaving a 30cm tail.

Re-thread the needle with the tail left after binding off, at the top of the glove, and begin seaming from the top until there is a gap of 6cm between the top and bottom side seams, which forms the thumb hole. Weave in all ends.

 GREENWOOD HAT

This warm winter hat features a number of interesting construction techniques, but is simply knitted with no need to purl. The two-colour hat band is knitted sideways in two-row garter stitch stripes which have similar elastic properties to ribbing, whilst also being very warm and insulating. The hat band is knitted flat, back and forth, and left unjoined, with a small rounded-edged button flap with two simple button holes forming a pleasant decorative detail. Stitches are picked up along the edge of the two-colour garter band and joined to knit in the round, culminating in classic spiral decreases for a neat finish.

MATERIALS

- Mirasol Sulka: 2 × 50g skeins of main colour, 1 × 50g skein of contrast colour
- Two coordinating buttons, 1.5cm in diameter

NEEDLES

- 6mm (US size 10) 50cm long circular needle
- 6mm DPNs for working decrease portion at crown (or substitute your favourite method of small-diameter knitting)

NOTIONS

Large, blunt-ended tapestry needle for sewing up

GAUGE

- Stitch gauge: 14 stitches per 10cm in stockinette stitch in the round
- Row gauge: 19 stitches per 10cm in stockinette stitch in the round

FINISHED MEASUREMENTS

Made to fit average adult with 47cm–52cm head circumference

ABBREVIATIONS

- MC = main colour
- CC = contrast colour
- sts = stitches
- c/o = cast on
- k = knit
- kfb = knit front and back (increase). Knit into the front leg of the stitch without dropping it from left needle, then knit into the back leg of the stitch.
- k2tog = knit two together (decrease). Knit two stitches together with the right needle, as if they were a single stitch.
- y/o = yarn over. Bring working yarn forward between the two needles, ready to knit the next stitch.
- b/o = bind off

SKILLS NEEDED TO COMPLETE THIS PATTERN

- Casting on
- Knit stitch
- Knitting in the round
- Knitting with two colours to form stripes
- Yarn overs
- Increasing (kfb)
- Decreasing (k2tog)
- Picking up stitches from an edge

INSTRUCTIONS

Using CC and circular needle, c/o 10 sts. The hat band is knitted back and forth on the circular needle.

Rows 1 & 2: Knit.

Row 3: kfb, k8, kfb (12 sts).

Rows 4 & 5: Knit.

Row 6: k2, k2tog, y/o, k4, y/o, k2tog, k2.

Rows 7–10: Knit.

Note: when swapping colours for garter stitch stripes, always be sure to bring new colour from under the old colour. This will form a decorative twisted edging to the brim of the hat.

Row 11: Swap to working with MC, knit all stitches.

Row 12: Knit.

Row 13: Swap to working with CC, knit all stitches.

Row 14: Knit.

Rows 15–154: Repeat rows 11–14 35 more times. When row 154 is reached there will be a total of 36 MC rows visible.

Row 155: Cut CC yarn, leaving a 30cm tail. Using MC, bind off all stitches until one stitch remains on the right-hand needle, but do not cut yarn.

Hold brim with the working yarn emerging from the top right corner and the buttonhole tab on the left.

Starting at the right-hand corner, pick up and knit one stitch in every garter stitch ridge until a total of 72 stitches have been picked up. Do not pick up stitches from the edge of the button tab.

Distribute stitches along the length of the circular needle, and ensuring the correct side is facing outwards, join to knit in the round.

Rounds 1–12: Knit.

Round 13: (k10, k2tog) 6 times. (66 sts)

Rounds 13–15: Knit.

Round 16: (k9, k2tog) 6 times. (60 sts)

Rounds 17–18: Knit.

Round 19: (k8, k2tog) 6 times. (54 sts)

Rounds 20 & 21: Knit.

Round 22: (k7, k2tog) 6 times. (48 sts)

Rounds 23 & 24: Knit.

Round 25: (k6, k2tog) 6 times. (42 sts)

Round 26: Knit.

Round 27: (k5, k2tog) 6 times. (36 sts)

Round 28: Knit.

Round 29: (k4, k2tog) 6 times. (30 sts)

Round 30: Knit.

Round 31: (k3, k2tog) 6 times. (24 sts)

Round 32: Knit.

Round 33: (k2, k2tog) 6 times. (18 sts)

Round 34: (k1, k2tog) 6 times (12 sts)

Round 35: (k2tog) 6 times. (6 sts)

Break yarn, leaving a 30cm tail. Thread a blunt-ended tapestry needle with this yarn tail and thread the needle through each of the six stitches still on the knitting needles. Pull the yarn tail tight to draw these stitches together and close the top of the hat. Weave in all ends and block hat if desired.

🐞 WINTER CUDDLES SET 🐞

This cosy set comprises a hot water bottle cover and mug cosy: perfect for keeping warm on the inside as well as out. Knitted in an easy-care wool and acrylic mix, this set is easily washable should any tea-spillage occur.

Cosies can be functional as well as decorative, especially when used for insulating purposes. The coffee cosy will keep hands protected from the heat of the mug whilst also keeping the drink hotter for longer. Similarly, the hot water bottle cover protects skin from the harshness of the water bottle's heat, whilst helping it to maintain its warmth for a greater length of time. A rugged, rustic tweed-style yarn has been chosen for this design, making this a perfect gift for a man as well as for a woman.

MATERIALS

- Stylecraft Life Super Chunky, 2 × 100g balls (125g needed to complete hot water bottle cover; 25g required for mug cosy)
- 4 × 15mm buttons for the hot water bottle cover and 3 × 15mm buttons for the mug cosy
- 50cm length of smooth round elastic is required for the mug cosy
- Coordinating sewing thread and needle for attaching buttons and button loops

NEEDLES

10mm (US size 13) straight needles

NOTIONS

Large, blunt-ended tapestry needle for sewing up

GAUGE

- Stitch gauge: 10 stitches per 10cm in stockinette

- Row gauge: 13 stitches per 10cm in stockinette

ABBREVIATIONS

- sts = stitches

- c/o = cast on

- k = knit

- p = purl

- yo = yarn over

- k2tog = knit two together

- p2tog = purl two together

- b/o = bind off

- RS = right side

- WS = wrong side

- C4F = Cable 4 forward. Slip two stitches to cable needle and hold at front of work; knit three stitches from left needle then two from cable needle.

- C6F = Cable 6 forward. Slip three stitches to cable needle and hold at front of work; knit three stitches from left needle then three from cable needle.

- C6B = Cable 6 backwards. Slip three stitches to cable needle and hold at back of work; knit three stitches from left needle, then three stitches from cable needle.

SKILLS NEEDED TO COMPLETE THIS PATTERN

- Casting on
- Knit and purl stitches
- Yarn overs
- Simple decrease: k2tog
- Simple cabling
- Binding off
- Sewing up and attaching buttons

Hot water bottle cover instructions

This hot water bottle cover is made in two parts (the front and the back) and then sewn together.

Back

Loosely c/o 22 stitches.

Rows 1–5: Knit.

Row 6 (RS): Knit.

Row 7 (WS): Purl.

Repeat rows 6 and 7 until work measures 29cm and ends with a WS (purl) row.

Shape the 'shoulders' of the cover:

Shaping row 1: b/o 5 stitches and knit to end of row. (17sts remain)

Shaping row 2: b/o 5 stitches and purl to end of row. (12 sts)

Knit the ribbed 'neck' portion of the cover:

Ribbed neck row 1: (k1, p1) 6 times.

Repeat this row until ribbed neck section measures 10cm.

Bind off all stitches loosely.

Front

Loosely c/o 22 stitches.

Rows 1–5: Knit.

Row 6: k2, k2tog, YO, k3, k2tog, YO, k4, YO, k2tog, k3, YO, K2tog, k2.

Row 7: (k5, kfb) 3 times, k4.

Rows 8–11: Knit.

Row 12: p4, k6, p5, k6, p4.

Row 13: k4, p6, k5, p6, k4.

Row 14: p4, C6F, p5, C6B, p4.

Row 15: k4, p6, k5, p6, k4.

Repeat rows 12–15 until work measures 29cm and ends with a RS row.

Set up row: (p5, p2tog) 3 times, p4.

Shape the 'shoulders' of the cover:

Shaping row 1: b/o 5 stitches and knit to end of row. (17sts remain)

Shaping row 2: b/o 5 stitches and purl to end of row. (12 sts)

Knit the ribbed 'neck' portion of the cover:

Ribbed neck row 1: (k1, p1) 6 times.

Repeat this row until ribbed neck section measures 10cm.

Bind off all stitches loosely.

Sew together two sides of hot water bottle cover using mattress stitch (pages 76–78) and attach buttons to finish.

Knitted in very chunky yarn, the hot water bottle cover is a quick project to complete. However, for the knitter who is really in a hurry to make a quick gift, the accompanying mug cosy can be completed in next to no time.

MUG COSY INSTRUCTIONS

Loosely cast on 8 stitches.

Rows 1–5: Knit.

Row 5 (WS): k2, p4, k2.

Row 6 (RS): k2, C4F, k2.

Row 7: k2, p4, k2.

Row 8: Knit.

Repeat rows 5–8 until work measures 20–21cm, ending with row 8.

Knit 4 rows.

Bind off all stitches loosely.

Attach three buttons to one short end of the mug cosy, one near each corner of the cosy and one in between these two. Cut elastic into three pieces. Fold each piece of elastic in half, along its length, and tie a knot about 3cm in from the 'bend' of the loop. The knot can be secured with a few stitches of sewing thread or a dab of superglue if desired. Trim ends. Using sewing thread, attach these loops to the wrong side of the cosy, at the opposite short end to where the buttons have been attached.

🐞 VIVIANNE SCARF 🐞

This airy, elegant scarf is surprisingly warm as it is knitted in a beautifully soft and warm cashmere blend yarn. Perfect for long spring walks, it looks equally at home draped around an evening outfit. Made from only a single skein, the easy-to-memorise simple lace pattern makes the most of a luxury yarn purchase.

MATERIALS

Skein Queen Blush, 100g

NEEDLES

5mm (US size 8) straight needles

NOTIONS

Large, blunt-ended tapestry needle for sewing up

GAUGE

Stitch gauge: 18 stitches per 10cm in wheat lace pattern, but gauge isn't too important in this pattern.

ABBREVIATIONS

- sts = stitches.

- c/o = cast on

- k = knit

- p = purl

- pm = place marker

- k2tog = knit two together (decrease). Knit two stitches together with the right needle, as if they were a single stitch.

- ssk = slip, slip, knit

- y/o = yarn over. Bring working yarn forward between the two needles, ready to knit the next stitch.

- b/o = bind off

SKILLS NEEDED TO COMPLETE THIS PATTERN

- Casting on

- Knit stitch

- Yarn overs

- Decreasing (k2tog, ssk)

- Binding off

INSTRUCTIONS

Loosely cast on 39 stitches.

Rows 1–5: Knit.

Row 6: k3, pm, knit 33, pm, k3.

The markers note the three stitch garter border at either side of the lace. Slip markers when they are reached.

Row 7: k3, *(k2tog) twice, k3, (ssk) twice, repeat from * 2 more times, k3.

Row 8: k3, p21, k3.

Row 9: k3, *k2, (YO, k1) 3 times, YO, k2, repeat from * 2 more times, k3.

Row 10: k3, p33, k3.

Repeat rows 7–10 until knitting measure 160cm long. End with row 10.

Knit five rows and loosely bind off all stitches. Weave in all ends and block to open out lace pattern.

🧶 BANDY LEGS SOCKS 🧶

These socks are the perfect all-round sock pattern. Available in a wide range of sizes, they are knitted in smooth stockinette with a ribbed cuff and professional-looking short-row heel and toe, which allow for both comfort and a good fit.

This pattern teaches short rows and the 'wrap and turn' method in a simple and easy-to-understand way, and is a fantastic way to learn this helpful shaping technique.

SIZES

- 17cm (21.5cm, 25.5cm)
- Measure around widest part of foot and widest part of ankle and use the larger of those two measurements.

MATERIALS

- Eskimimi Knits 'twingles' yarn, 1 set
- One set contains two 50g skeins of yarn twisted together. The knitter should decide which is their main colour (MC) and contrast colour (CC).

NEEDLES

2.75mm (US size 2) DPNs, set of five

NOTIONS

Blunt-ended tapestry needle for sewing up

GAUGE

- Stitch gauge: 28 stitches per 10cm in stockinette (in the round)
- Row gauge: 38 stitches per 10cm in stockinette (in the round)

ABBREVIATIONS

- sts = stitches
- c/o = cast on
- k = knit
- p = purl
- MC = main colour
- CC = contrast colour

SKILLS NEEDED TO COMPLETE THIS PATTERN

- Cast on
- Knit and purl stitches
- Knitting in the round (on DPNs)
- Short rows
- Kitchener stitch

INSTRUCTIONS

Using MC, loosely c/o 56 (64, 72) stitches, dividing stitches equally between four needles. There should be 14 (16, 18) stitches on each needle. Join to knit in the round, being careful not to twist the cast-on edge.

Knitting the cuff
Rounds 1–8: (k1, p1) around.

Change to CC

Rounds 9–16: (k1, p1) around.

Knit the leg
Change to MC

Rounds 17–64: Starting with MC and swapping yarn colour every eight rows, knit 48 rows in stockinette stitch (knitting every stitch). You should end with 8 rows of CC.

Knit the short-row heel

Change to MC and begin knitting the short row heel. The short row heel is knitted back and forth over only the first two needles, using only the first 28 (32, 36) stitches. You will be ignoring the stitches on the third and fourth needles for a while and so may wish to place these stitches on a stitch holder or spare piece of yarn while you knit, if you find it more comfortable to do so.

Row 1 (RS): Knit until last stitch, bring yarn forward between needles, slip last stitch to right needle, bring yarn back to rear of work, slip stitch back to left needle. There is now a 'wrap' around the base of the last stitch. Turn work.

Row 2 (WS): Purl until last stitch, take yarn backwards between needles, slip last stitch to right needle, bring yarn to front of work, slip stitch back to left needle. Turn work.

Row 3: Knit until one stitch before nearest 'wrapped' stitch, bring yarn forward between needles, slip last stitch to right needle, bring yarn back to rear of work, slip stitch back to left needle. Turn work.

Row 4: Purl until one stitch before nearest 'wrapped' stitch, take yarn backwards between needles, slip last stitch to right needle, bring yarn to front of work, slip stitch back to left needle. Turn work.

Repeat these last two rows until you have 10 (12, 14) unwrapped stitches in the centre of your short row sections.

Change to CC for the remainder of the short row heel. The next part of knitting the short row heel involves re-knitting over your wrapped stitches, picking up the wraps as you go, and working one further row each time.

Row 1: Knit to the first wrapped stitch, slip that stitch to the right needle. Using the tip of the left needle, pick up the wrap. Place the slipped stitch back on to the left needle, alongside the wrap. Knit the stitch and its wrap together, through the back loop. Bring yarn forward between needles, slip last stitch to right needle, bring yarn back to rear of work, slip stitch back to left needle. Turn work.

Row 2: Purl to the first wrapped stitch, slip that stitch to the right needle. Using the tip of the left needle, pick up the wrap. Place the slipped stitch back on to the left needle, alongside the wrap. Purl the stitch and its wrap together. Take yarn backwards between needles, slip last stitch to right needle, bring yarn to front of work, slip stitch back to left needle. Turn work.

Row 3: Knit to the first wrapped stitch, which now has two wraps. Slip that stitch to the right needle. Using the tip of the left needle, pick up both wraps. Place the slipped stitch back on to the left needle, alongside the wraps. Knit the stitch and its wraps together, through the back loop. Bring yarn forward between needles, slip last stitch to right needle, bring yarn back to rear of work, slip stitch back to left needle. Turn work.

Row 4: Purl to the first wrapped stitch, which now has two wraps. Slip that stitch to the right needle. Using the tip of the left needle, pick up both wraps. Place the slipped stitch back on to the left needle, alongside the wraps. Purl the stitch and its wraps together. Bring yarn backwards between needles to rear of work, slip last stitch to right needle, bring yarn forward between needles, slip stitch back to left needle. Turn work.

Repeat rows 3 and 4 until all wraps have been knitted together with their stitches.

Knitting the foot

The knitting of the sock will now continue in the round. If the stitches from needles 3 and 4 were placed on a stitch holder or spare yarn, now is the time to place them back on to the needles. Change to MC.

Knitting stockinette in the round (knitting every stitch) and switching colours every eight rounds as before, knit the foot section of the sock. Continue knitting every round this way until your work from the colour change mid-way through the heel measures 4cm less than your actual foot length.

Knitting the toe

The toe is knitted in exactly the same way as the heel. It is recommended that you change yarn colour from the last band of colour you knit for the foot and knit the entire toe in that colour, rather than changing at the half-way point.

Finishing

When the toe is complete, place stitches from needles 1 and 2 on to a single DPN. Place stitches from needles 3 and 4 on another DPN. There will be 28 (32, 26) stitches on each needle. Kitchener-stitch these two rows of stitches together for a smooth, invisible finish to your sock. Weave in all ends and block.

6

IT'S ALL IN THE DETAILS: EMBELLISHMENTS

Often, it is the choice of detailing that can make a piece. Small elements of stylish embellishing can add just a little panache to an otherwise plain knitted garment, and take a hand-knitted piece a step above the mass produced items on the market.

KNITTING EMBELLISHMENTS

Some forms of knitting embellishment take place during the knitting, through the use of decorative knitting techniques such as lace knitting or the use of cables, whilst other methods of embellishing knitwear take place after the knitting of the garment is complete, by adding haberdashery items such as decorative buttons, closures, knitted corsages and appliqué patches, or by embroidering and decorating the surface of the knitted fabric.

Choice of embellishments can really give a sense of individuality to a piece, whether through the restrained use of classically elegant buttons or a far more flamboyant use of surface decorations by a knitter who is not afraid of gilding the lily.

Many knitwear designers seek to give their designs an 'edge' by adding interest to the knitted fabric of their finished piece. Whether through the inclusion of colourwork, lace panels or the twisted rope-like stitches typical of cable knitting, decorative knitting techniques not only make for an interesting garment but also an interesting knitting project.

✂ CABLE KNITTING ✂

Cabling is one of the most popular ways of adding interest to a knitted piece, and is easy to achieve with the use of a handy little tool known as a cable needle. Not to be confused with a circular needle which comprises two needle ends and a flexible cable, a cable needle is a short double-ended needle between 10cm–15cm long, usually with a bend or kink along its length.

Pocket Fact ☺

Some knitted cable work can look amazingly intricate and complex, but no additional lengths of yarn are needed to create the decorative forms. Cables are produced simply by knitting the established stitches out of their regular order, creating twists in the surface of the fabric.

The cable needle is used to hold a number of stitches 'in waiting' whilst knitting a cable. A small number of stitches are slipped on to the cable needle, and with the stitches secure upon this needle, it is allowed to hang at the front or back of the fabric whilst a small number of stitches are knitted from the left needle. The waiting stitches are then knitted directly from the cable needle, so creating a 'twisted' area of stitches on that row. When arranged in formation, these twists can be used to form beautiful and intricate patterning within the fabric.

Pocket Tip ✄

Whether the cable needle stitches are held at the front or back of the work whilst cabling determines the direction that the cable will twist in. If the cable needle is held to the front the cable will twist to the left, if it is held at the back the cable will be right-twisting.

Most cable patterns do not involve working cable stitches on every row, and many will only require the knitter to make a twist with the cable needle every four or six rows (or more), depending on the intricacy of the cable pattern being used. The technique can be used to generate a lot of effect for only little effort.

Pocket Tip

One thing to bear in mind when experimenting with cables is that the twists in the knitted fabric cause the width of the knitted piece to contract, so a heavily cabled piece of knitting will require a greater number of stitches to be cast on to achieve the same width of knitting than if the knitter were knitting the same garment in stockinette stitch. This is taken into account when knitting from published patterns from designers, but needs to be considered if the knitter is modifying a plain knitted garment to incorporate their own cable embellishments.

Knitting patterns will almost always specify the way to knit the cable stitches they incorporate: how many stitches to slip to the cable needle, whether the cable needle should be held at the front or back of the work and if the stitches should be knitted or purled to complete the cable.

The Winter Cuddles hot water bottle cover and mug cosy gift set pattern on pages 127–131 makes use of simple cabling, and is a great project to experiment with this interesting knitting technique as the cables add bulk and therefore added insulation, and are often associated with a feeling of cosiness.

DECORATIVE LACE KNITTING

At the opposite end of the knitting texture scale to cable knitting is the light and decorative technique of lace knitting. Creating an eyelet in a piece of knitting is extremely simple. A yarn over, as well as being used as an increase, makes a small 'hole' in the knitted fabric. Often paired with a decrease stitch (to keep the stitch count consistent), these yarn over holes can be used us a decorative detail. A row of yarn overs and decrease stitches can form a decorative row of eyelets. If arranged in more complex patterns and combined with different directional decreases, however, these simple eyelets can combine to form complex lace patterns of breathtaking beauty and delicacy.

Pocket Fact ☺

One knitting heirloom tradition is the knitting of wedding ring shawls. These usually circular shawls are knitted in very fine gossamer weight lace yarn and, despite their large diameter, are fine enough to pass through a wedding ring.

Items that might not be functional if made entirely from delicate lace might instead be given decorative detailing in the form of a lace panel or other decorative lace embellishment on collar or cuff. The restrained use of lace panels in this manner can add interest to otherwise plain knitted items, such as socks and cardigan collars.

Pocket Fact ☺

Some knitters make a distinction between what they term 'true' lace and other lace patterns. In these terms, true lace describes lace patterns that have lacy yarn over stitches on every row, including the 'wrong side' rows. Many lace patterns have the knitter purl every wrong side row.

LACE LIFELINES

Some knitters feel overwhelmed at the thought of attempting large or complex lace patterns, worried about the consequences of making a mistake or dropping a stitch a long way into the pattern, as it can be a lot more difficult to pick up stitches or fix errors in a complex lace pattern. Prevention is better than cure when knitting lace, and the use of a lifeline is recommended. A lifeline is a length of smooth yarn or embroidery floss that is passed through every stitch of a row of knitting when working on a lace pattern. To insert a lifeline whilst knitting, simply thread a blunt-ended tapestry needle with a length of yarn or embroidery floss and thread through each and every stitch on the needle.

Pocket Tip ✀

Dental floss is an inexpensive, strong and smooth alternative to using yarn for lifelines and has the added benefit of making the project smell pleasantly minty.

Lifelines should be added as often as the knitter feels necessary. If a mistake is discovered and deemed too difficult to fix, the knitting can be ripped back to the previous lifeline and the inserted thread will catch the row of live stitches, ready to replace them on to the needles so knitting can resume from the saved row.

Lace stitch patterns are often used to make elaborate shawls and other decorative garments, but some of the most effective lace patterns are quite simple to knit. The Vivianne Scarf (pages 132–133) uses a simple, repetitive and easy to remember lace stitch to great effect and makes an excellent simple lace project.

❀ COLOURWORK ❀

Any piece of knitting that involves the use of more than one colour for decorative effect can be termed 'colourwork'. From the most basic stripes, to the picture-like knits of the intarsia method (see page 145), through to the intricate and colourful forms of stranded patterns, colour can really bring a project alive.

STRIPES

The simplest form of colourwork is probably the humble horizontal stripe. By changing between two or more different-coloured yarns every few rows, the knitter can easily form bands of colour and knit their very own football scarf.

Pocket Tip

When knitting stripes, the knitter can decide whether to cut the yarn every time they begin a new stripe or to carry the not-in-use-colour up the side of the work. Cutting and joining in a new section of yarn for each colour change is recommended when knitting wide stripes as it makes for a neater edge, but also requires the weaving in of many ends.

FAIR ISLE AND STRANDED KNITTING

Another popular form of multi-colour knitting is that of Fair Isle (see page 86) and other forms of stranded knitting. Stranded colourwork involves the use of more than one colour per row, where the unused colour yarns are stranded across the back of the knitted piece, creating short floats of yarn. Stranded colourwork patterns usually feature short runs of colour, ensuring that the stranded lengths of yarn are kept short to prevent them snagging on fingers, buttons and jewellery.

Working Fair Isle and stranded knitting patterns

Stranded colourwork patterns are almost always presented in the form of the chart. Following the chart, knit each stitch with the required colour of yarn whilst keeping the out-of-use colours towards the back of the work and out of the way. When knitting two-colour stranded knitting, some knitters choose to tension each yarn colour in a different hand, using one hand to tension the yarn English and the other to tension the second yarn Continental style (see pages 31–32).

There are a few things you should bear in mind when working a stranded colourwork pattern:

● *Ensure that floats are not made too short, otherwise the colourwork will pucker.*

- *Choose a pattern that does not feature long rows of colour, so long yarn floats are kept to a minimum.*
- *When working a pattern that does feature long sections knitted in a single colour, twist the working yarn under the yarn not in use every five or six stitches, to hold the yarn floats against the back of the piece of knitting.*

INTARSIA

Another form of colourwork that produces a different effect entirely is that of intarsia, also sometimes known as picture knitting. Popular in the 1970s and 1980s, intarsia involves knitting short lengths of yarn into a graphic pattern reminiscent of a picture. Each section of colour of the intended design requires a separate bobbin of yarn in a corresponding colour. Intarsia patterns are knitted row by row with the two bobbins of colour twisted together every time the edge of two coloured sections meet. Complex intarsia patterns may require the use of many tens of individual bobbins at any one time, and can require much patience when the bobbins become entangled. Intarsia projects are rarely chosen for a piece of simple, relaxed travel knitting but can produce beautiful results.

🐛 SURFACE EMBELLISHMENTS 🐛

Cabling, lace knitting and colourwork are all forms of decoration that are formed whilst the piece is still being knitted. Each of these techniques forms part of the knitting itself, with the decorative elements actually helping to form the fabric of the garment.

An alternative way to give further interest and decoration to a piece of knitting is to add surface embellishments once the knitting is completed.

Pocket Tip ✄

Ribbons, buttons, beads and many other items from metal washers to seashells can be sewn or otherwise attached to a completed piece of knitting, and a haberdashery stall represents a veritable Aladdin's cave to the knitter with a little flair and imagination.

EMBROIDERY

Embroidery is a whole craft within itself, but simple embroidery stitches can be used to give beautiful detail to a piece of knitwear. Surface embroidery can be made using either yarn or specialised embroidery flosses, or even a narrow length of ribbon. Each material will give a different effect, but can be used for great impact. Books of embroidery stitches are quite easy to find in any good book store, but there is also a wealth of information on simple embroidery techniques to be found on the internet using the search term 'embroidery stitches'.

NEEDLE FELTING

Another form of surface decoration often favoured by fibre enthusiasts is that of needle felting. This variation on the craft of felting involves using a sharp (very sharp) barbed needle to push loose fibres down amongst the fibres of the knitted piece. This works because under a microscope the surface of wool is not smooth but instead covered in tiny microscopic scales. When fibres are tangled together these scales lock on to each other and hold the individual strands of fibre in place. The barbed needle felting tool helps to push these fibres down into the knitted piece, making them 'lock' in place. Needle felting can be used to apply either un-spun fibres or spun yarn to a piece of knitting and is especially effective when used to apply designs to a felted piece of knitting.

FELTING

Heat, water and agitation are the three ingredients needed to turn a piece of knitting into a piece of felt. Felting an item can be a heart-stopping moment when done accidentally and the delicate and detailed jumper that took so many weeks to knit is removed from the washing machine resembling a jumper for a chihuahua, and so stiff it will barely fold in half. When done on purpose, however, turning a knitted piece into thick wool felt can provide stability and insulation to make anything from shapely hats to warm and cuddly hot water bottle covers.

FULLING

The process of fulling a knitted item can be a rather uncertain affair. There are no guarantees of how much an item might shrink or thicken and what the resulting size or dimensions will be. The rule to follow when fulling a hand knit is to check the process every five minutes and to stop as soon as the right level of fulling has been achieved. Much like whipping cream, the process can seem like it is doing nothing at all for absolutely ages, and then in a flash the cream has turned to something resembling butter and the knitted item is as thick as a mattress.

Pocket Fact ☺

When a pre-knitted piece of fabric is shrunk and thickened using heat, water and agitation to form a piece of felt, the process is properly known as fulling. Many knitters will refer to the process as felting but the two resulting fabrics do differ slightly in form, as felt is composed of separate fibres that have been interlocked together to form fabric, whereas a fulled item is already formed before the felting process begins.

Fulling can be done by hand or in the washing machine. Put the item into warm water with a tiny amount of soap and agitate by either squeezing the water through the fibres in the sink or by adding heavy items such as an old trainer, pair of jeans or even a couple of tennis balls when using the washing machine. Remember to check and re-check every five minutes until the item has taken on the appropriate dimensions. Do not spin-dry felted items as it will cause creasing, and dry the items over a hard form to make sure that the finished object dries in the correct shape.

Pocket Tip

Not all fibres will full. Non-Superwash wool, alpaca and llama are a few of the fibres that will usually give good results when fulling, but other fibres such as acrylic and cotton will not. Superwash wool is wool that has been specifically treated to prevent shrinkage and so is not recommended for fulling. See page 9 for more on Superwash wool.

BAUBLES AND TASSELS

Other popular knitwear embellishments include those made from yarn. As knitters enjoy working with yarn and tend to have quite a bit of it hanging around the place, pompoms and fringes are a quick and easy way of adding a bit of fun to a garment.

Pompoms

These fluffy balls of yarn best known for sitting atop bobble hats are easily made using only some yarn and a couple of pieces of cardboard.

1. *Draw around something circular, such as a mug or roll of sticky tape, on to one piece of card and cut out that circle. Draw a smaller circle in the centre and cut this out, leaving a doughnut of cardboard. Trace around this on to a*

second piece of cardboard and place both doughnuts of cardboard together.

2. *Wind lengths of yarn through the centre hole and all around the outside of this cardboard doughnut until the card is covered with a generous layer of yarn.*

3. *Using a sharp pair of scissors, snip at the outside edge of the cardboard circles, cutting through all the strands of yarn until all the lengths of yarn are held in the centre circle.*

4. *Use another length of yarn to pass between the two cardboard doughnuts and encircle the bundle of yarn in the centre and tie into a tight knot before removing the two cardboard rings.*

FRINGES

Fringes are even easier to make, with the use of a crochet hook and a few lengths of yarn. Simply insert the crochet hook from front to back through the edge of the knitted piece. Fold a length of yarn twice as long as the intended fringe in half and catch the loop on the crochet hook to draw it through to the front. Pass the two ends of the strand through the loop and pull the ends to draw tight. Strands of yarn can be added one at a time or in 'bundles' for a fuller fringing

DEVIATING FROM RECOMMENDED EMBELLISHMENTS

Embellishments and decorations are often what give individuality to a knitted piece, so do not be afraid to experiment with unusual buttons or colours that deviate from the pattern photograph. Knitting is all about fun and making garments that are special to the knitter and the wearer, and if it turns out that those clown-car buttons do look a bit strange on grandad's cardigan, they can always be removed and swapped for something a little more sedate.

Pocket Tip ✄

Lengths of yarn all of the same length can be quickly and easily made by wrapping a long length of yarn around a book and then cutting through the end of the strands of yarn to provide many strands of the same measurements.

7

WHEN IT ALL GOES WRONG: FIXING MISTAKES

Most knitters will, at some point, feel like the knitting gods have turned against them as they stare in despair at what must surely be a cursed project. The most important thing to do when this happens is to remember that it happens to even the best knitters. Nobody's knitting is perfect all of the time, and mistakes will happen. Sometimes a mishap may be terminal for the project, but more often than not a piece of knitting can be rescued. Before that sweater back is launched across the room at high velocity it is worth seeing if the piece of knitting can be salvaged.

🧶 DROPPED STITCHES 🧶

One of the most common knitting errors is a dropped stitch. They occur quite easily — a stitch slips off either needle without being noticed and several rows later is discovered to have gone off on a wander down the piece of knitting, creating a 'ladder'. That stitch can be coaxed back with a little bit of know-how, some patience and a crochet hook.

Pocket Fact ☺

Intentionally dropped stitches and their resulting ladders are features of some open-textured patterns. Dropping stitches on purpose can seem both quite liberating and a little bit nerve-wracking at the same time.

PICKING UP KNIT STITCHES

The first thing to do with a dropped stitch is to stop it dropping any further, by poking the end of a spare knitting needle, pen lid or whatever else is to hand until a rummage in the knitting bag produces a crochet hook. Knit until the spot directly above where the dropped stitches begin. Take a calming breath and begin to pick up the dropped stitches:

- Place the tip of the crochet hook through the loop of the bottommost dropped stitch, from front to back.

- There will be a line of horizontal 'bars' resembling the rungs of a ladder (hence 'laddering') above the dropped stitch. Use the crochet hook to pull the bottommost of these bars through the loop on the crochet hook, so creating a new stitch. There is now one stitch picked up and a new loop on the hook.

- Pull the next bar through this loop and continue upwards until the top of the knitting has been reached. Slip the loop from the hook on to the knitting needle.

Pocket Fact ☺

Women's nylon tights are a form of knitted fabric on a very fine scale. When a single thread of this fine knitting becomes broken it acts like a dropped stitch, and causes the minutely knitted fabric to 'run' or 'ladder'.

PICKING UP PURL STITCHES

If the dropped stitch has occurred whilst knitting the reverse side of a piece of stockinette fabric, it is usually easier to turn the piece of knitting over and pick up the stitches from the knit side. However, with some textured pieces of knitting a combination of knit and purl stitches may need to be rescued. To pick up a purl stitch:

- Place the tip of a crochet hook through the loop of the bottommost dropped stitch, from back to front.

- Catch the bottommost 'bar', just as with picking up a knit stitch, but this time pull it through the loop on the hook and towards the reverse of the knitting. Continue in this manner until all dropped stitches have been picked up and the top-most stitch is returned to the knitting needle.

✖ MISSING AN INSTRUCTION ✖

Sometimes a knitter will become distracted from their knitting by conversation or a particularly engaging scene in a movie, and may miss a knitting instruction as laid down by the pattern. To fix mistakes like this it is often best to un-knit back to where the mistake has occurred and re-knit the stitches according to the pattern.

Pocket Fact ☺

Un-knitting is sometimes known as 'tinking'. 'To tink' a piece of fabric is to undo the knitting a single stitch at a time, and the word 'tink' comes from it being the reverse spelling of the word 'knit'.

TINKING

As knitted fabric is created, stitches are moved from the left needle to the right, with new yarn being added to create new stitches. Tinking reverses both of these actions, undoing that yarn and placing the stitches back on the left needle. To tink stitches:

- Place the tip of the left needle into the loop below the first stitch on the right needle. Slip the stitch off the right needle and give the working yarn a little tug. This will undo the new stitch.

- Repeat until the area where the mistake occurred has been reached.

UNRAVELLING

Every once in a while a knitter will notice an error further down their knitting that is perhaps too complex or too far down to be salvaged with tinking, and a slightly more drastic form of action may be required. In these cases it may be necessary to unravel, or pull back a number of rows. The trick to successfully unravelling several rows of knitting without the unravelling getting out of control is to take it slowly and not pull angrily at the knitting out of frustration.

Pocket Tip

Some mohair-type yarns are difficult to unravel, as the fine fluffy hairs like to grab on to each other once knitted. Putting the project in the freezer for half an hour or so is believed by many people to aid with the unravelling process.

To unravel a piece of knitting, simply slide all of the stitches off the needles and pull gently at the end of the yarn, re-winding it on to the ball as it is freed from the knitting. Once the mistake has been unravelled, all of the stitches should be placed back on the needles and knitting resumed.

Pocket Tip

To save unravelling more than is intended, thread a blunt-ended tapestry needle with smooth strong yarn or a length of embroidery floss. Pick out a single row of stitches below the row that the mistake is on and pass the needle and yarn under the left 'leg' of each V-shaped stitch. Make sure to keep to a single row of stitches and to pass the needle through each and every stitch. Once all stitches of this row are safely on the yarn, remove the needles from the knitting and unravel the yarn. When you reach the row of stitches with the line of yarn running through them they will all be held in place, ready to re-insert the knitting needle.

🪡FROGGING🪡

Sometimes the best thing to do is admit defeat. It happens to even the most experienced knitters and has to be accepted rather than feared. Sometimes a piece of knitting just isn't 'working'. It may be due to an irrecoverable mistake, or it may be because the knitter slowly comes to a realisation that they don't like the combination of yarn and pattern that they have selected. Perhaps it is because it becomes apparent half way through the project that the sweater that's being worked isn't going to fit the intended recipient, or perhaps the knitter just isn't enjoying that particular piece of knitting. All of these scenarios are reason to embrace the inner amphibian and enjoy a good 'frog'.

To frog a piece of knitting means to pull out your work, often with wild abandon, to either restart that particular piece or to reclaim the yarn for use in future projects.

Pocket Fact ☺

The term 'frogging' or 'to frog' comes from the alternative term for unravelling large areas of work – to 'rip out' your knitting. The idea of this comes from the desire to gleefully pull out large areas of knitting, with the desire to 'rip it, rip it!' – which sounds like the ribbiting of a frog.

Frogging a project can sometimes seem like a deflating course of action, but it is worth remembering that the yarn can be used for other (and better things), and that it is worth undoing the knitting and starting again if it means that the knitter will end up with an even more wonderful end product. Knitters should perhaps see frogging as an activity that liberates both the yarn and the knitter and as the first step to new knitting possibilities.

☀ MISTAKE? WHAT MISTAKE? ☀ OTHER IDEAS FOR FAILED KNITS

If a knitter has a piece of knitting that will not work for its original purpose but which they simply cannot stand to frog, either due to the time and work involved or because they have made, despite everything, an attractive piece of fabric. In these cases the knitting may be able to be re-purposed. Here are a few ideas:

- Use a sewing machine and a small, close stitch to sew a 45cm square around a sweater back. Leaving a 2cm allowance, cut around this line to make an attractive square of fabric to turn into a cushion or bag.

- Pure wool or high-percentage, non-Superwash wool items can be lightly felted and sewn into all manner of objects such as toys and purses. Once the fabric has been felted the edges can be cut with no fear of fraying and either sewn up or left 'raw' (unfinished).

- Items felted to a higher degree can be cut into 10cm squares to make drinks coasters, or larger rectangles to make potholders.

Pocket Fact ☺

Fundraiser and knitter Susie Hewer managed to knit a 120cm long scarf for charity whilst also running a full marathon.

GLOSSARY

4-ply
British yarn weight, equivalent to 'fingering weight' or 'sock weight'.

Acrylic
Popular man-made fibre; washable, easy care (see page 10).

Alpaca
Fibre or yarn from the alpaca, an animal of the camelid family, which gives luscious, silky, warm fibres (see pages 12–13).

Angora
Fibre or yarn from the angora rabbit. Extremely soft and fuzzy (see page 13).

Aran (knitting)
Textured pattern knitting, traditional to Ireland's Aran Isles (see page 85).

Aran (yarn)
British yarn weight, equivalent to a US heavy 'worsted' weight and Australian 12-ply.

Art yarn
Yarn spun with an unusual structure or inclusions, such as beads, ribbon or found items such as sea shells. Usually produced in small, often unique, batches by independent spinners.

Ball band
Information label on a ball or skein of yarn, detailing fibre content, recommended needle size and recommended gauge (see page 19).

Ball winder
Device used for winding hanks of yarn into centre-pull balls.

Bamboo
Rayon fibre or yarn, sourced from bamboo (see page 2).

Blocking
Finishing technique which uses water or steam to 'set' stitches into place. Blocking can be used to great effect in lace knitting, where it is used to increase the size of knitted pieces and 'open up' the decorative lacy stitches (see pages 73–75).

British yarn weight system
This uses the term 'ply' to refer to yarn thickness. A 4-ply weight yarn may contain only one actual ply.

Bulky
Description of yarn weight. Thick yarn, good for quick projects; also known as chunky or 14-ply.

Cable
Twisted, rope-like texture stitches made by knitting stitches out of regular order, using a cable needle (see entry below).

Cable needle
Short double-ended needle, often with a bend or 'crook' in its length, used for holding stitches in waiting when making cables.

Cashmere
Fibre or yarn from the cashmere goat. Usually expensive, and a luxury fibre (see page 13).

Chunky
Description of yarn weight. Thick yarn, good for quick projects; also known in Australia as 14-ply.

Circular (knitting)
Knitting in the round; produces cylindrical pieces of knitting for items such as hats, socks and sleeves.

Circulars (needles)
Two short needle tips joined by a smooth, flexible cable, used for circular knitting.

Cobweb
Description of yarn weight. Extremely fine yarn used for sheer lace knitting.

Colourwork
One of several forms of knitting that involve working with different colour yarns to produce patterned knitted fabric. Colourwork can be as simple as changing yarns to produce stripes, to stranded knitting techniques such as Fair Isle, or inset picture work techniques such as intarsia.

Continental
A knitting method in which the working yarn is tensioned with the left hand. Also sometimes known as 'left-hand knitting' though this does not denote its suitability or otherwise for left- or dominant right-handed knitters.

Cotton
Fibre or yarn from the cotton plant (see page 11).

Crochet
Fibre craft that, like knitting, uses yarn to create pieces of fabric.

Crochet hook
Tool used to crochet with. A handy addition to the knitting bag for embellishment, picking up stitches and, of course, crocheting with.

Decrease
One of a number of stitches used to make a piece of knitting narrower.

DK
British yarn weight, short for 'double knitting'. Equivalent to light worsted or sport weight yarn.

DPN (double pointed needles)
Short (12cm–20cm) needles with two pointed ends, for knitting in the round; sold in sets of four or five.

Drape
The way a piece of knitted fabric hangs – how fluid the folds of fabric fall when hanging.

'Dropped' stitch

Said of a stitch when it has fallen off the needle, especially if it has travelled down several rows, creating a 'run' or 'ladder'.

Ease

The size of a garment in relation to the person it is intended for. (See also positive ease, negative ease and page 92.)

English

A knitting method in which the working yarn is tensioned with the right hand. Also sometimes known as 'right-hand knitting', though this does not denote its suitability or otherwise for left- or dominant right-handed knitters.

Entrelac

From the French *entrelace*, meaning to interlace or interweave. Entrelac knitting produces a diamond-patterned, textured knitting with the appearance of woven strips. Entrelac knitting is completed one small diamond at a time, picking up a row of stitches to join the pieces together.

Fair Isle

Originating from the Fair Isle, part of the Shetland Isles, this is a stranded knitting technique recognisable by traditional motifs in bands of colour.

Felt/Felting

Fabric created by the interlocking of woollen fibres. This can be achieved with friction, water or heat. When applied to the deliberate shrinking of knitted fabric the correct term is fulling.

Fingering

Yarn weight, equivalent to British 4-ply weight or sock weight yarn.

Finishing

The tasks such as blocking, seaming, weaving in of ends and attaching of buttons, which 'finish' a knitting project.

Floats

Strands of unused coloured wool that sit across the back of a piece of knitting when doing stranded colourwork.

Frogging
To unravel whole sections of knitting. The term 'frog' comes from the wish to pull or 'rip' vigorously at the kitting, so giving rise to the phrase 'rip it, rip it!' – which sounds like a frog's croaking call.

Fulling (to full)
The correct term for intentionally felting a piece of knitted fabric.

Garter stitch
Simple knitting stitch that produces horizontal ridges.

Gauge (knitting)
A gauge swatch is a knitted square used to measure how many stitches the knitter is getting per 10cm; used to ensure that the garment will turn out to be the correct size. (See also swatch definition on page 167.)

Gauge (needle)
Tool, often resembling a ruler, with various-sized holes drilled in it, used for measuring needles to ensure they are the correct size.

Give
The stretchiness of a piece of fabric. A firm, dense piece of knitted fabric has very little give in it, whilst a stretchy and elastic piece of knitting has a greater degree of give.

Grip
The amount of friction between a needle and yarn. Different fibres and needle materials affect how much grip (sometimes 'grab') is experienced. A slippery yarn and slick needles produce very little grip, whereas a rugged yarn and micro-textured needles will produce quite a lot of grip.

Hank
Loop of unwound yarn, ready to be wound into a ball.

Increase
One of a number of stitches used to widen a piece of knitting.

Intarsia
Sometimes known as 'picture knitting', intarsia is a form of colourwork in which each individual colour is held on a bobbin

and knitted in place, twisting yarns together at a colour change. Usually used for large motifs.

Interchangeables
Sets of needles comprising several cable lengths and needle tips, which can be swapped on and off to make a large range of circular needle sizes.

In the round
Circular knitting, which produces cylindrical pieces of knitting for items such as hats, socks and sleeves.

Kitchener
Method of invisibly joining two live sets of stitches straight from the needles, using a tapestry needle. Often used for the toes of socks and on shoulders to provide a comfortable and invisible join.

Lace (knitting)
A form of knitting in which deliberate 'holes' (formed by a combination of yarn overs and decreases) are arranged to form intricate patterns.

Lace (yarn)
Very fine weight yarn used mostly for lace knitting.

Ladder
A vertical line of dropped stitches, caused by one dropped stitch travelling down previous rows.

Lanolin
From the Latin *lana*, meaning 'wool', and *oleum*, meaning 'oil'. A waxy, yellow substance secreted from the sebaceous glands of wool-bearing animals such as sheep. Used in many beauty products and added to some woollen garments to provide waterproofing.

Lifeline
Length of smooth yarn or embroidery floss passed through a row of stitches whilst knitting lace. Used to recover a row of stitches should the knitter make a mistake.

Linen
Fibre or yarn produced from the flax plant; popular in summer wear (see page 15).

Magic Loop
A method that uses a long circular needle to knit small-diameter objects in the round by manipulating the patch of the cable and distribution of stitches.

Marl
Yarn made from different coloured strands of yarn twisted together in barber-pole fashion; produces fabric with a highly flecked appearance.

Mattress stitch
Method of invisibly joining two pieces of fabric, especially used for side seams and when working in stockinette.

Merino
Fibre or wool from the merino sheep – a particularly prized breed of sheep producing soft and warm wool (see page 9).

Modular knitting
A form of knitting from which fabric is produced from small blocks of knitting which have been joined together, either by picking up stitches along one or more edges as each new block is added, or by joining separate blocks together after the knitting is complete.

Mohair
Lustrous fibre or yarn from the Angora goat. Not be confused with angora yarn, from the Angora rabbit (see page 13).

Moss stitch
Knit and purl stitches arranged in a checkerboard pattern to form a pleasant texture and flat-lying fabric. Also called seed stitch (see page 56).

Negative ease
The degree to which a tight-fitting garment hugs the body. If the measurement of a sweater is 5cm smaller than the measurements of the person it is intended for, it is said to have 5cm of negative ease. (See also 'Ease'.)

NiddyNoddy
Simple wooden tool used for making yarn into hanks.

No ease
The degree to which a tight-fitting garment hugs the body. A sweater knitted with no ease will be close-fitting without being tight. It will follow the lines of the body but will not be restrictive. (See also 'Ease'.)

Nostepine
Simple wooden tool used for hand-winding yarn into centre-pull balls.

Notions
Additional knitting tools needed to complete a project.

Pick/Picking (knitting style)
The knitting action used by many Continental-style knitters, so named as the needle is used to catch hold of (or 'pick') the working yarn.

Pick up/Picking up
Either to rescue dropped stitches or to pull a line of stitches through an already formed piece of knitting, such as when creating a new piece of knitting perpendicular to an existing piece of knitting to create button bands, etc.

Picture knitting
Another name for intarsia. A form of colourwork in which each individual colour is held on a bobbin and knitted in place, twisting yarns together at a colour change. Usually used for large motifs.

Plarn
Yarn made from plastic shopping bags.

Ply
A single twisted 'strand' of fibre. Several plies are usually twisted together to form a length of yarn, though single-ply yarns do exist. Not to be confused with the British yarn weight system, see earlier entry.

Pooling
When areas of a multi-colour ball of yarn line up to form large pools or blotches of colour.

Positive ease
The degree to which a loose-fitting garment is larger than the body. If the measurement of a sweater is 5cm larger than the measurements of the person it is intended for, it is said to have 5cm of positive ease. (See also 'Ease'.)

Private side
The side of a piece of knitting not intended to be seen by the public (often the inside). Some pieces of knitting (such as many scarves) have no 'wrong' side. Also called 'wrong side' (WS).

Public side
The 'right' side of a piece of knitting, or the side that everyone is supposed to see. Some garments, such as many scarves, have two public sides and so are a good use of double-sided stitch patterns. Also called 'right side' (RS).

Rib/Ribbing
Knitting stitch composed of vertical columns of knit and purl stitches, which contract to form a very elastic fabric.

Right side (RS)
See 'Public side' above.

Schematic
Diagram outlining the shape and measurements of individual pieces of knitting and how they should be joined together.

Sewing up
The process of joining knitted pieces into a finished garment.

Short rows
A shaping technique in which not all the stitches of a row are knitted. Often used for bust and shoulder shaping, as well as for forming the heels and toes of socks.

Silk
Fibre or yarn produced from the cocoons of the Bombyx silk moth. A fine and lustrous fibre (see page 12).

Skein
Sausage-shaped pre-wound yarn. Many people use the word 'skein' to refer to any way of packaging yarn, whether it be wound into a ball, hank or actual skein. Pronounced to rhyme with 'cane'.

Slipperiness
The measure of how slick a pair of needles or type of yarn is. Slippery needles and yarn allow the knitting to glide quickly and smoothly over the needles.

Sock yarn
Yarn made specifically for socks, but which can be used for other items such as shawls and scarves. Sock yarn often contains 10%–30% nylon content for greater wear and durability, and is often Superwash to allow for easy machine laundering. Most often manufactured in 4-ply/fingering weight, though 6-ply socks yarns are also available.

Sport weight
American yarn weight, equivalent to British 5-ply weight or DK (double knitting yarn), and Australian 8-ply. Can be difficult to source in the UK. A light DK weight or heavy fingering weight yarn could both act as substitutes.

Steeking
A method in which a piece of knitted fabric is reinforced with two lines of sewn or crocheted stitches before the knitting is cut. Often used with stranded colourwork when creating the open front of a cardigan, or splitting the centre of a V-neck sweater. This allows the jumper to be knitted in the round, so avoiding working stranded colourwork on the wrong side.

Stockinette/Stocking stitch
Simple knitting stitch that typically produces a very smooth flowing fabric with good drape.

Straights (needles)
Traditional, single-point knitting needles with a finial on the end.

Stranding/Stranded knitting
Stranded knitting techniques involve using more than one colour to knit a pattern. Colours not in use are 'carried' across the back of the knitted piece, creating short strands or floats (see 'floats' above).

Superwash
Yarn which has been chemically treated to make it resistant to felting/shrinking when machine-washed (see page 9).

Swatch
Square of knitting used to measure how many stitches-per-inch the chosen needle and yarn are giving, to make sure they match the selected pattern. Essential in achieving properly fitting garments. Also sometimes called a 'tension square' or gauge.

Swift
Simple rotating tool used to hold a hank of yarn whilst it is being wound into a ball. Can resemble the arms of a windmill or the metal innards of an umbrella canopy.

Tension
The 'tightness' of the knitted stitches in a piece of fabric. Adjusting needle size results in a change of tension should the tension need to be adjusted to knit at the correct gauge.

Three-needle bind off
A bind off technique which uses a third needle to knit together and bind off two live sets of stitches. Often used on shoulder seams and occasionally for sock toes.

Throw/Throwing
The knitting action used by many English-style knitters, as the yarn is manipulated (thrown) around the needle.

Tink
The word 'knit' backwards, meaning to undo stitches one at a time, maintaining the knitting on the needles the whole time.

Tweed
Rustic-looking yarn with small flecks of colour.

Unravel
To undo knitting by pulling on the yarn end.

Variegated
Yarn with small sections of various colours produced by dyeing techniques.

Weight (yarn)
The weight of a yarn does not refer to how many grams or ounces it weighs, but to its bulk or thickness. A heavyweight yarn is chunky and thick, and a lightweight yarn is fine and thin.

Wool
The natural fibre obtained from the coat of the sheep which is shorn, cleaned and spin into yarn (see pages 7–8).

Worsted (yarn weight)
Yarn weight equivalent to a heavy DK weight or light Aran weight in the UK.

Wrong side (WS)
See 'Private side' above.

Yarn
Material used to knit with.

Yarn store
A neighbourhood yarn shop.

CENTIMETRE-TO-INCH CONVERSION CHART

If you'd prefer to work in inches rather than centimetres, here's a handy conversion chart. Make sure you only work in centimetres *or* inches.

Centimetres	Inches
1	0.4
2	0.8
3	1.2
4	1.6
5	2
6	2.4
7	2.8
8	3.2
9	3.6
10	4

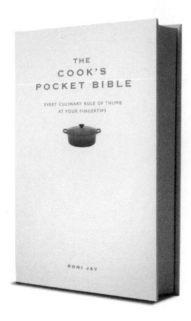

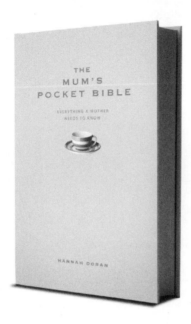

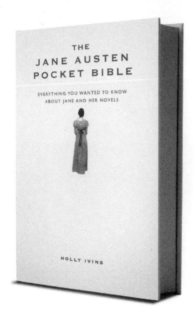